Anyone But Celtic

Inside The Culture That Created The Lanarkshire Referees Association

By
Paul Larkin

ISBN 978-1-326-12815-9
© 2015 Paul Larkin

Also by the same author:

Books:

The Football Club: Celtic first, last and always (2002-out of print)

Planes, Trains and Martin O'Neill (2003-out of print)

From Albert, With Love (2011)

Dougie, Dougie (2011)

Wim's Tims (2011)

Albert, Dougie and Wim (Compendium of previous three books- 2012)

Poles 'N' Goals and Hesselink (2012)

By Any Means Necessary: Journey with Celtic Bampots (2012)

The Last Pearl Diver (2013)

The Asterisk Years: The Edinburgh Establishment versus Celtic (2013)

Short Stories that have appeared in print:

Coasters (2008)

When you Yank a Metropolitan (2013)

Soundtrack of the New York Waterfall (2013)

Films

The Asterisk Years (2014)

Future Projects

Anyone but Celtic (Film, 2016)

E********* (Book, 2016)

P***** D****** (Film, 2017)

Website:

www.ls86productions.com

Twitter:

@Paullarkin74

Facebook Group:

'Paul Larkin Books'

This book is dedicated to Jill, for helping me get in the zone and stay there.

Foreword – Page 9

Note from the Author – Page 13

Preface – Page 15

The Fiefdom of Jack Mowat – Page 37

Just Another Saturday – Page 55

The Carluke Connection – Page 67

At Our Expense – Page 89

When Jim Was Foiled By Albert – Page 99

Freemasonry and the Lanarkshire Referees Association – Page 121

The Dallas Cowboys – Page 137

A Fish Rots From the Head Down – Page 157

That's Why We're Paranoid – Page 179

Don't Call it a Comeback – Page 193

Epilogue – Page 219

Bibliography – Page 241

Thanks – Page 243

Foreword by John Fallon

How can you not be part of the Celtic family when we have fans like Paul, he has stood up against the establishment with his last book and film, *The Asterisk Years*, now he takes them on again.

In this book he tackles the what I call them the Lanarkshire Mafia, but at Hampden it's called the Scottish Referee's Association,

That's polite but at a game well that's another story well with our fans and other fans, these people who make honest mistakes most weeks are above reproach, it's "I never saw it" or "my back was turned away" , well that doesn't stand with me cause we know one referee that gave a penalty with his back turned.

But let Paul take up his story people will call him bias, bigoted, as if not for first time, this story is an eye opener, yes about honest mistakes against our club from when we were formed. Yes that's how long it has been going on.

I can remember my Grandfather, Father and eldest brother schooling me on our history and of course mistakes, thinking back, there have been plenty for our young readers you will be amazed at what went on not just recently but since our history began.

When Paul asked me to meet him for a "quick chat" about this book it lasted 3 hours, I was giving him tales from the dark side, of penalties given or not seen, of refs we knew were against us, how Jock handled some, of players getting ordered off for kicking a ball that hit a ref.

It all happened.

Yes there are some who will criticise what's in this book saying that refs are human and make mistakes yes they do but not as much as against Celtic FC,

Sit back, enjoy this book and think of the trophies we lost out on.

Hail Hail
John Fallon
Celtic FC

"If you have a dog, I must have a dog. If you have a rifle, I must have a rifle. If you have a club, I must have a club. This is equality."

Malcolm X

Anyone but Celtic
By
Paul Larkin

> **FOOTBALL.**
>
> SCOTTISH FOOTBALL LEAGUE. — The usual monthly meeting of the First Division Committee was held last night, under the chairmanship of Mr Montgomery, Third Lanark. The chief business was Celtic's protest against Rangers in connection with the New Year's game, on the ground of the referee's incompetency (Mr Nisbet, Edinburgh), and full time not being played. After hearing the referee, who stated that full time was played, the protest was dismissed. For repeatedly refusing to answer a question arising out of the said match, the Committee deleted Mr Nisbet's name from the referee list. Cathkin Park was unanimously chosen as the venue of the Inter-League game against Ireland.
>
> ENGLAND v. WALES.—At the last moment it is announced that J. Daniell (Cambridge University), the captain of the English team, is unable to come back from Cairo in time to take his place, so the vacancy will be filled by the inclusion of S. G. Williams (Devon), a splendid forward with a rare turn of speed.

Note from the author

The paragraphs that appear in italic indicate that they have been sourced from elsewhere, not spoken to me and written entirely by someone else. A full bibliography appears at the end of the book.

Preface

It is my opinion that the man who suffered most from the relentless cheating and bias Celtic have faced in my lifetime was Tommy Burns. As player, manager, first team coach, head of youth development and scout (not to mention as good an ambassador Celtic have ever had) no one has given Celtic more in my lifetime. It is often said that Tommy was so much of a supporter that it clouded his judgement as a manager. I find that a bit odd, this is a man who went through an entire season with Celtic losing only one game, and yet people question his managerial skills? It is also my opinion that Tommy Burns started the modern day Celtic we all know. Jock Stein unquestionably lifted the club to Olympian heights but there is no doubt by the early 90's the club was stagnating as latterly Billy McNeill then Liam Brady, Joe Jordan (albeit for a day) Frank Connor and Lou Macari struggled to make any on field impact. Tommy came in and restored pride in the supporters and put a team on the park that played the Celtic way. He was one of us.

One of my inspirations for this book is the incestuous relationship between the Grand Lodge of Scotland (The Masons) and the Grand Orange Lodge of Scotland (The Orangies) and their continuous polemic, deleterious resentment for anyone not like them. Masons round the world are different to those in Scotland. I visited Masonic temples in Melbourne, Perth WA, Philadelphia, Los Angeles, London and Lisbon. All I met there were open, affable, polite people happy to talk about "The Craft" (Most of it making them sound like a Church of Scotland Sunday School it has to be said) In Scotland I reached out to all the lodges in Lanarkshire, no one responded to emails or rung me back. In Edinburgh I was told I could look inside the George Street building (Something I can so any time they host a Record Fair there) but no one would talk. I accept that maybe some of them know what I am about and want as much do to with me as, well, I want with them but they do give the impression they have something to hide.

I also reached out to all Loyal Orange Lodges in Lanarkshire, asking for interviews (had I been granted any I'd have taken Jason Higgins and 10 guys just like him) but again, no response was forthcoming. Funny, because this comes at a time when the Orange Order is seemingly reaching out to the populous. They even had an 'Orangefest' in George Square, Glasgow on June 6th 2015 where they expected 50,000 people to turn up. On the day it was under 2000 who braved the festival. Interestingly enough, one of the billed star performers was Pastor Mike McCurry, a former Referee who was accused of being biased for Rangers.

Now there's a thing.

In Scotland, it's acceptable to be a Mason and Referee, despite the obvious connections between the masons and the Orange Order in Scotland. Connections that see similar memberships, similar structures, similar meetings in similar halls containing the same people. Yet we are to believe they are completely different?

This relationship is Scotland's NRA/KKK.

The book focuses on the most secret part, the Grand Lodge of Scotland, particularly some of its Lanarkshire members.

This book also looks at people who achieve leadership status in the game. It is important, I feel, to look at who has been in charge of various things in Scottish football over the years to show what kind of character rises to the top in the game in Scotland.

This is also another book about cheating. In sport, cheating is the worst thing you can do. On any level. It doesn't really matter how it's done, merely that if it is done, all bets are off. Or on as the case may be. In *The Asterisk Years* we saw one form of cheating, financial doping, and in this book we see another form, institutionalised bias.

I guess the first time I ever heard clarification of cheating in Scottish football was in 1994. Rangers had brought out a cassette tape to celebrate an anniversary of the now dead club and on it came the startling admission from Rangers player, Bobby Brown about a referee: *"Queen of the South had never beaten Rangers, and they had a corner on the right very near the end. I asked the referee how much time was left, and he said, 'you're alright: it's time up after this corner.' A header by Jim Paterson of the home side found the net, but was promptly disallowed. George Young took the resulting free kick, and the referee blew the final whistle immediately afterwards. Two years after that, I was privileged to attend a presentation at a lodge for that referee, and in his speech of thanks he said that in eighteen years of football his proudest boast was that he had never refereed a losing Rangers team"*

My late father, Jim The Tim, always brought up two days that, in his mind, summed up the feeling towards Celtic in Scotland. On January 1st 1969, Celtic beat Clyde 5-0. Nothing unique to that. Except on January 2nd 1969, Celtic lost 1-0 at Ibrox after being forced by the SFA to play two games in 24 hours. To compound matters the Rangers goal, scored by John Greig, was a penalty that was given after a ball struck Billy McNeil on the chest, clearly indicated by the mark on his jersey.

That night the announcer on BBC Scotland said '*Here is the result all Scotland has waited for...Rangers 1-0 Celtic.*'

Scottish football's attitude towards Celtic and its players has remained the game forever and a day. People who deny it has ever been one of disdain and outright prejudice never really look at the facts nor indeed want to hear them. Things like Britain's top scorer ever, Jimmy McGrory, getting a measly seven caps for Scotland. Or the Lisbon Lions, Scotland's greatest ever team, getting a total of 114 caps between them whilst the Rangers team they consistently swept aside was given a total of 155 caps. Kenny Dalglish was inexplicably dropped when about to play his 34th game in row for Scotland. I say inexplicably but when I tell you he would have broken George Young of Rangers consecutive cap record, it's not that inexplicable. Jimmy Johnstone, Danny McGrain, Davie Hay, Roy Aitken, Brian McClair and Paul McStay were all targeted by sections of the Scotland support when they played and Aitken and McClair were also targeted by sustained media campaigns designed to ensure their removal from the squad.

Celtic players who played against Scotland were often targeted and indeed, as someone who went to Scotland games regularly from 1983 onwards, I stopped going after a Scotland versus Poland in May 1990. I had gone to see the team get off the bus at Hampden and heard Alan McInally get a torrent of abuse as he got off the bus. I'd always had a soft spot for Rambo and said "Good Luck" to him as he went in. As he turned to me he was clearly in tears and just said "Thanks". Then during the game, Polish Celtic player, Dariusz Dziekanowski was subjected to a constant barracking given with as much gusto as "Mo, Mo, Super Mo" was sung by fans who would have despised said Mo a year previous.

I believe because that attitude flourished in Scotland it allowed institutions like the Lanarkshire Referees Association to grow strong.

Celtic supporters get many insults thrown at them. I get a shitload too. Indeed this book, and I, will get lots of them. For instance, I guarantee some of the reviews for this book will carry some abuse. They will say I am paranoid, a crap writer, deluded, a schemie tramp and all sorts of other jolly stuff. There will be a couple that will even be outraged that I have dared to write another book and will burst a blood vessel battering the keyboard trying to ensure you don't buy this book. This book is not about me though. Most of these insults, collectively, we now are able to hit back at immediately, but the one that has been thrown at them for decades now is the point of interest for this book: Paranoia. That's not to say this book is aping the Tom Campbell book *Celtic Paranoia: All in the Mind?* This book is designed to peel back the curtain a little on an institution that was able to construct a recruitment policy where a certain mind set would be able to flourish. That mind set is one Celtic supporters are well used to encountering, simply put it is the one that would have anyone but Celtic win football matches. This is something that makes fans of smaller teams in Scotland recoil, as they cite the "Big clubs get all the decisions" mantra. That's fair enough, it's true in the main. Except in Scotland where the biggest club in it has suffered continuous bias from people who are paid to be impartial.

You'll see a lot of repetition of names and places at the beginning of this book. This was completely inspired by David Peace in his book *Red or Dead* and in a chat I had with him in Edinburgh in August 2014 where we discussed repetition in football. I thought it applied to referees and how often we, as fans, saw them, and how they were always described up until the last few years. I'm sure you'll get what I mean and it's only to join their name with places in areas of the book I feel appropriate.

Finally, one thing inspired this book more than anything or anyone else, the source. This is a man with intimate knowledge of the Lanarkshire Referees Association and the Scottish Football Association and the inner workings of both. This man saw all the main players in these organisations, the way they operated, how they ran things, who moved chairs, sold raffle tickets, organised functions, chaired meetings, manipulated the powerful and greased the pole of careerism. The Lanarkshire Referees Association is a branch of the SFA but in reality it is the refereeing wing of the SFA with other associations holding little or no power within the SFA. Virtually all the famous refereeing names in Scotland over the last 55 years rose through the ranks of the LRA and the source of this book knew them all. That's important because it allows for the veil of secrecy to be unmasked.

Secrecy is important to the LRA. Primarily because of its incestuous relationship to the Grand Lodge of Scotland, in particular it's lodges based in Carluke, Wishaw and Rutherglen.

"Who's the mason in the black?" is chant often emanating from Celtic supporters all over Scotland, this book will point them out.

Incidentally, *The Asterisk Years* had an incredible source and one that I will always protect. I actually took a ton of shit for not outing that source or taking the story to the tabloids. I might be many things but I don't sell people out or sell my soul to the newspapers. Almost everywhere I went with *The Asterisk Years* people would ask "Why has this stuff not been in the press?" and I would answer "Do you go to Celtic games expecting the opposition striker to score goals for us?" Media has gone 180. Everyone is freelance and you build your own platform and keep getting higher. As *The Asterisk Years* became more successful I started getting more and more flak from my own kind. That is genuinely the only thing that ever hurts me. Some people took exception to my own experiences in Edinburgh being in the book as I strove for a comparison piece to highlight "Them and us" I had a lot of great feedback on it but some folk absolutely despised it. Win some, lose some. All I try to do is get the stories and books I write out there, even with the film of *The Asterisk Years* I did a Q&A at every screening to explain myself further. I do believe you have to go all out in any passion project but believe me you'll get a lot of shit. Thing is, you'll get a fuckload of support as well.

And Celtic has the best supporters in the world.

Passion is a funny thing actually, you rarely see it in the Scottish media unless it's journalists trying to whip people into a frenzy or when it's a fight on the Radio to see who has been the best at being subservient at Ibrox over their careers.

The key element here is we have been conditioned by a Hollywood meets Holyrood kind of narrative by a compliant media to believe the likes of the Serie A is corrupt without a second thought whereas in Scotland we are conditioned to believe that this sort of thing could never happen. Occasionally small clubs make honest administrative errors and the book is thrown at them by officialdom whilst journalists shake their heads and scream "Amateurism". Yet when huge clubs in Scotland, like Rangers for example, cheat their way through two decades and then liquidate because of it, the media act like the whole thing was a mirage of David Copperfield proportions. As the mouthpiece of power, journalists in Scotland play a key role in enabling corruption because of their continual refusal to partake in actual journalism in favour of the constant PR work that engulfs the media in Scotland. They churn out endless puff pieces on who gives them the odd exclusive whilst desperately painting a picture, one that Bob Ross would struggle with, that everything is rosy in the garden.

What these books try to do is fight back at that and show that Celtic supporters were not paranoid.

I've always been a Celtic supporter and always will be so accusations of bias will be thrown at me and this book will, no doubt, be dismissed as the ramblings of a paranoid Tim.

Similarly, I don't expect any journalist to pick this up or acknowledge it in public because their career means more than actually being a journalist.

With that being said, I am immensely grateful to you for buying this book and supporting what I do.

The stuff I've written in the past always had an autobiographical narrative running through it. There are many drawbacks to this kind of writing. Firstly, I never at any stage thought that people who didn't know any of the information I gave out in my books would read them. This leads to people you know absolutely nothing about knowing a shed load of stuff about you which puts you at a disadvantage in all sorts of situations, the weirdest of which was when I bit back at the actor James Woods on Twitter after he claimed people were poor because they didn't work hard enough. This led to, literally, thousands of right wing Americans attacking me non-stop on Twitter for around a month solid. I gave as good as I got to begin with but to answer everyone I'd have needed four more thumbs, three more phones, and a hell of a lot more patience. Then one day I noticed a spike in sales of my books in America on Kindle. I made about £6 a book from a sale of *The Asterisk Years* on Kindle, way more than a paperback copy.

Thinking no more of it, I started to notice a trend develop from a few of my Tea Party tantrum people. Abuse started to get more personal and these people started mention things like my failed marriages. Yeah, they bought my books, read them and then used personal stuff against me. A situation in my life I thought as likely to happen as Beyonce phoning me up and asking if I fancied a quick pint in The Gunner. The decent footnote is the money (£180 or thereabouts) I made from the books they bought I donated to The Kano Foundation. Thanks for paying it forward guys.

The other main drawback is that a lot of people don't want someone like me to write about their lives. There are two reasons for this, the first is a lot of people despise anyone with a working class background trying to do anything creative or positive. Especially in a class system like we have in the UK. I read Owen Jones book, *Chavs*, and it perfectly illustrated throughout the rising hatred of the working class in the UK. I've seen it all my life but have only experienced it when I tried to turn my life around. Nobody really cared what I did before then. The second is people like me, especially those who know me, can think "Why has he written a book and not me?" I can tell them, I did it, that's the only reason. No other reason, I sacrificed a lot to do it, put in the hours and churned it out. Either way, those kind of questions can affect your mood, bring you down and ensure you waste lots of time dwelling on it. So I thought I'd put a bit in this book about it, which you've just read, and move on. At 41, I realised life is too short and although I will share some aspects of my life in this book, it's hard to write a factual book without doing this, it will be much, much less than normal.

I'd like to think my books have progressed from the rough fanzine style that I did want back in the day but can easily be mistaken as rank amateurism. Myself and Average Joe Miller used to always talk about having a sort of 'street' feel to the books and Chas Duffy used to always say to me "Keep it real" (*Sniffin' Glue,* the fanzine not the recreational habit, was also huge inspiration to me) I don't regret any of them but I do have issues with the book I did, *Dougie, Dougie,* because although I do think the message in it was right and came to pass ("Don't complain about the media, become it") it was essentially just a series of blogs that I'd already written and even though the money from the book went to the Thai Tims, I quickly amalgamated it with *From Albert, With Love* and *Wim's Tims* so folk got their money's worth. Don't take that as a dig anyone, anywhere who has put out books of blogs either, I don't care what anyone else does in that regard. I don't get any kick out of slagging others work no matter what they say about me or how good or bad their work is. I don't mind the format either (I've actually bought all of Kevin Smith's books which are essentially that format. I'm babbling on now, sorry)

Anyway, back in the summer of 2013, I thought I'd write do a sort of journal of the season for no other reason than to keep me busy. Writers all over the world will say you should always keep a journal but I only tried it once, back in the summer of 2005 and it lasted about three months. Primarily because I thought Gordon Strachan would drive me mad. The other thing writers do is when they don't have an idea, they think just putting out their own thoughts, opinions and musings is exactly the thing that world has been waiting on. Speaking as someone who wrote about lots of aspects of my life I feel I can comment with some qualification. The stuff I wrote had two rules attached: The first was to edit out the boring stuff and the second, believe it or not, was to edit out the really nasty stuff. The first rule was simple, I wasn't, and will never be, confident enough to think anyone wants to read about me going to the shops, doing the washing or endlessly scrolling Twitter. The second was more complicated, I've not been a paragon of moral virtue all my life, some may think that even now and that's fine. However I would be writing about situations which could compromise others and that's a no-no for me. So I left out parts like when I coached a women's softball team in New Jersey, when I was doing podcasts in Manhattan as far back as 2006 and when I was a dealer in Long Island City.

Of course, in summer 2013, *The Asterisk Years* turned my life on its axis and exploded in my mind so therefore it occupied almost every day of my life for the next two years in some shape or form. So the journal never happened is what I am saying. I found myself in a similar situation about a year later when something came along that blew me away just like the story of the Edinburgh Establishment had. It was a story of another establishment who, just like the one in Edinburgh, lived within a bubble where they effectively had their own rules, operated with impunity and created a world that lived under the radar.

Until now.

I guess then this book is part three of a loose trilogy (*By Any Means Necessary* and *The Asterisk Years* being parts 1&2)

The Lanarkshire Referees Association won't be known to many outside Lanarkshire but it has grown, cultivated and ran some of the most important men in Scottish football for decades. It has had a vice like grip on the SFA for over 50 years now, it has a recruitment policy which includes Masonic initiations and membership, its social events are planned so as not to clash with big Masonic events and it has a membership of which 75% are Masons. Its big names, past and present, read like a who's who of Scotland's refereeing elite, Don McVicar (Carluke), Bobby Davidson (Airdrie), Ray Morrison (Carluke), George Cumming (Carluke), Bobby Tait (East Kilbride), Jim McCluskey (Airdrie), Hugh Dallas (Bonkle), Willie Collum and Euan Norris (Carluke).

So I guess what I am saying is I've given up writing about aspects of my life for entertainment purposes (whether it be yours or mine), focusing now on experiences related to the subject matter and am now writing about others so I've became another writer leech. I hope it works for you. It does for me.

Oh and those things I mentioned that didn't go in previous books? Softball was for one night when a friend "stood down" the existing coach, the podcasts were for a CSC and members only so aren't "out there" and it was cards not drugs.

So why did I pick this topic and that association to write about?

Well, that association has one goal:

To ensure anyone but Celtic win football matches in Scotland.

So how to go about it? Well, some background was in before I really discovered how to write this book. I didn't want to write this book full of stories about my life, as I've already said, but I felt the unravelling of it, and the wider "Anyone but Celtic" attitude which still exists was as much part of this story as Hugh Dallas (Bonkle) or George Cumming (Carluke) are.

Paul Larkin
August 2015

March 13th, 7.24pm, Airdrie (The Pitch)

I feel like I should pitch this book to you and that it should start in Airdrie. I'm sitting in Airdrie town hall on March 13th, 2015 (Check the calendar, that's Friday the 13th in Airdrie) and *The Asterisk Years* is showing. I'm well into a tour that has made me comfortable about who I am and what I am doing. It's a noisy, boisterous tornado-like crowd that is about to watch the film on the biggest screen it has ever been shown on. I'm not worried though, this film has rendered the loudest, maddest audiences so quiet that you could hear a church mouse piss. That worried me at first but they say silence through a film is the best compliment it can get. I say "They", it was actually Mark Kermode that did on the radio one day. A week before tonight, it dawned me that I better get back into the new book, this book, but I still didn't have the right angle to do it from. The night before I thought that, I'd been in Winchburgh showing the film and I could read the signs, the equipment hadn't been checked until the night of the screening and the sound wasn't working. A lot people stood about as if surveying the scene of an accident and brows got more furrowed as the night wore on. The hall was packed and the natives were restless. And drunk. The equipment worked eventually and the film started but it was two hours late which meant I'd be doing a Q&A two hours later than normal and that's not a good idea. However the guys running the show are really good guys and I didn't want to let them down. I can sense trouble a mile away and my senses were strong. To my left, maybe five yards from me, there was a guy scowling at me. Every time I answered a question, he had his own narrative and it was getting worse and worse. I ignored it for about half an hour until I clearly heard him say "I'll kick your cunt in" to me. I was mid answering a question and was going to ignore it when he moved one step towards me. So I turned round and said "try it". I shouldn't have done that but I'd had this guy in my ear for half an hour now and I'd had enough. Of course folk looked stunned and he repeated the threat so I told the committee to get him out of there. Red mist had descended and the reason I wanted him out was so I could follow him.

That was daft of me.

It was all calmed down and the guy was tossed out. So, what's this got to do with anything? I woke up the next day and realised I'd had a wake-up call. The film had exceeded all expectations and I was enjoying the adulation. I'd never had this level before and I was loving it. A bad place for a writer to be. I knew I had to get the head down and start moulding this book into something that got right to the heart of the matter. People who cheated Celtic for decades weren't born that way, this society created them and it was this society I had to explore as well as the Lanarkshire Referees Association.

I text my main source on this and asked him to come to Airdrie. He was very sceptical, particularly when he heard what was happening that night, but agreed to come. I had another friend coming that night too so I hoped that would cloak him a little. I also told him not to sit next to me or be obvious. As the story centred in and around Lanarkshire, I wanted it to start in Lanarkshire and, I have to say, segue from a film screening. Airdrie is a place that I'd passed through many times on the train and had visited to watch Celtic play there at Broomfield, old and new, but I'd never spent any real time there.

Something had struck me around March 2014 when I visited Coatbridge the year before to do a book talk (and no, it wasn't a missile from the audience) but I couldn't quite put my finger on what it was. I'd been back in Coatbridge the week before the Airdrie event, twice in actual fact and I got the same feeling again. I put it down to a Coatbridge welcome until I got to Airdrie and felt it again. I looked around the huge town hall where the film was showing and studied closely. I looked at all the faces in the hall and they reminded me of Coatbridge. I saw glimpses of this all over the world, Tommy and Frankie at The Fenian Bhoys in Manhattan have it, Paddy McOnie in Perth, WA has it, Chris Broadley in Wimbledon has it, Scott Richards in Philadelphia has it. Many people have it in fact but collectively I'd seen so much of it in one place as I had in Coatbridge. Now I was seeing it again in Airdrie. What was it?

Defiance.

There was something else that happened that night too.

I was sitting chatting with one of the Airdrie Bhoys when Tom Boyd approached me. It's wasn't the first time an ex Celtic player has approached me within *The Asterisk Years* project but it was the first time someone from my era had. It was a magical moment because he said "I really want to see this film" and I could have gone to meet my maker right there, right then, happy. Are you kidding me? The captain of the team that stopped 10 in a row?

Moments like that make me realise we are all in this together and have to stick together.

See it is clear to me now more than ever that aspects of Scotland's society were designed to ensure that people of a certain background could not prosper in life. This book will outline a lot of these obstacles but to flip it round and provide both further scope and evidence, because there are Celtic supporters who left the UK and then prospered having never really previously done so. The sort of obstacles they faced abroad are the normal ones anyone faces, getting work, finding a home, a partner and being happy not ones like when the ex-Celtic player Lex Baillie joined the police force and a Celtic supporting detective was told "That's you oot the fitba team, Lex will fill our Tim quota instead" with no hint of sarcasm.

It's why, when news broke in June 2012 that Glasgow City Council would be funding the Orange Lodge's Jubilee celebrations it came as no real surprise to most Republicans and/or Socialists in Scotland. Early in 2000 it was discovered that West Lothian Council was giving Orange flute bands a "Culture Grant" to travel over to the occupied six counties of Ireland so they could lay siege to Catholic areas in the north. Sinn Fein were able to expose it and get it stopped but the fact that in the modern day this attitude still exists is both shocking and unsurprising. You could wonder about the mind-set of a council who thinks this is a route they should be going down. You wouldn't wonder too long though because the well-worn traditional route is summed up with one phrase "We are The People"

That phrase sums up a lot of life in Scotland and why things are why they are.

There's also a thing where every so often we are reminded why we must be defiant. The club, Celtic, can feel under siege at times with a compliant media always willing to stick the boot in but, more importantly, deflect from the real issues.

These stories and books are always designed to tell a different narrative. I too have been a victim of press conditioning over the years, due in no small part to a desperation for success and have been sucked in before. For example, if you'd asked any Celtic supporter who travelled down on July 23rd 1997 to watch us play Inter Cable-Tel in Cardiff what our chances of success were in terms of stopping Rangers doing 10 in a row, I'd guess most would say about the same as Oasis and Blur going for a pint together. The Celtic team that took the field that night, Marshall, McNamara, Stubbs, Boyd, Hannah, McKinlay, Donnelly, Wieghorst, Gray, Thom, Johnson, may not have been the worst Celtic team ever but the subs of McCondichie, Morrison, Elliot, McBride and Jackson told its own story. We had an average team with an untried bench and Darren Jackson. I stood outside Celtic Park the day Jackson was unveiled, signed by Davie Hay it should not be forgotten, and certain journalists were briefing the supporters that it was Gianluca Vialli that was about to come out. When Darren came out the guy next to me said "Fur fucks sake they've signed Jackson anaw" but we all knew what was happening and when one guy booed, that became the story. We should have known but we didn't and the media had won again. Headlines of "Joke Brown" when Celtic appointed Jock Brown as General Manager were becoming common place about the club and after a summer long search for a manager ended with Wim Jansen being unveiled, the press greeted his arrival with "The second worst thing to hit Hiroshima" a dig at Jansen's previous unsuccessful spell in Japan. What wasn't printed by the Scottish press was the quote from Johan Cruyff who described Wim as "One of only four people in the world worth talking football with" I'm going to leap here and say the other three aren't Traynor, Keevins or Leckie. The team that started in Cardiff were without the "Three Amigos" of Di Canio, Cadete and Van Hooijdonk. Infighting, bitching, call it what you will, had become as much part of the Celtic culture as Glen Daly and with a salivating press always ready to print the anti-Celtic side of the story, almost every day we were treated to "Leetle Problems" emerging as Paolo would say. The crux seemed to be that all three were promised to be "looked after" if successful, they thought they had been, Fergus McCann said "Show me the trophies" and like that, they were gone, along with, it seemed, any chance we had of protecting our sacred nine in a row record of 66-74. Quite frankly the club were a shambles that summer. Everywhere. After the previous season, I'd gone to Dublin and London for three weeks to get away from it all but when I came back in mid-June I needed my Celtic fix so and went through to basically look at the stadium and buy something from the shop. I say shop, it was a porta cabin. In 1997 Celtic were in the process of building a superstore but it wasn't ready yet so when I went through there was said hut with one girl, some new training jerseys, pennants and no clue when the new top would be on sale. There was a queue of people at the ticket office for season tickets and the obligatory know-all steward who was telling everyone Di Canio was staying.

My whole mind set was conditioned by the tabloid press then as they add to a culture and society in Scotland.

The culture and society in Scotland that allows Celtic to be cheated with impunity.

Let's see why…

The Fiefdom of Jack Mowat

Medal won by Jack Mowat, Referee of European Cup Final, 1960

The European Cup was a foreign body to Scotland in 1960. It had been two years since The Busby Babes had suffered enormous tragedy, with Lanarkshire born Matt Busby almost losing his life when flight 609 failed on its third attempt at take-off from a slush filled Munich runway and 23 people lost their lives.

A lot of teams from Britain had thumbed their nose at the advent of the European Cup. The first edition of the European Cup took place during the 1955–56 season. Sixteen teams participated: Milan (Italy), AGF Aarhus (Denmark), Anderlecht (Belgium), Djurgården (Sweden), Gwardia Warszawa (Poland), Hibernian (Scotland), Partizan (Yugoslavia), PSV Eindhoven (Netherlands), Rapid Wien (Austria), Real Madrid (Spain), Rot-Weiss Essen (West Germany), Saarbrücken (Saar), Servette (Switzerland), Sporting CP (Portugal), Stade de Reims (France), and Vörös Lobogó (Hungary). The first European Cup match took place on 4 September 1955, and ended in a 3–3 draw between Sporting CP and Partizan. The first goal in European Cup history was scored by João Baptista Martins of Sporting CP. The inaugural final took place at the Parc des Princes between Stade de Reims and Real Madrid. The Spanish squad came back from behind to win 4–3 thanks to goals from Alfredo Di Stéfano and Marquitos, as well as two goals from Héctor Rial.

As well as noticing Hibs representing Scotland, it also stands out that no English team participated in the first competition. There was a suspicion coming from England regarding 'Johnny Foreigner' with to regards to pretty much everything then and this extended to football. Chelsea had originally been penned to play in the European Cup of 1955/56 but had been persuaded by the Football League not to participate. Indeed it was Matt Busby's

Babes at Manchester United who became England's first ever entrants the following season.

Real Madrid successfully defended the trophy next season in their home stadium, the Santiago Bernabéu, against Fiorentina. After a scoreless first half, Real Madrid scored twice in six minutes to defeat the Italians. In 1958, Milan failed to capitalize after going ahead on the scoreline twice, only for Real Madrid to equalize. The final held in Heysel Stadium went to extra time when Francisco Gento scored the game-winning goal to allow Real Madrid to retain the title for the third consecutive season. In a rematch of the first final, Real Madrid faced Stade Reims at the Neckarstadion for the 1958–59 season final, easily winning 2–0. In season 59-60, West German side Eintracht Frankfurt became the first non-Latin team to reach the European Cup final

Real Madrid 7 Eintracht Frankfurt 3
Real Madrid: *Rogelio Domínguez; Marquitos, Pachín, José Santamaría; José María Vidal, José María Zárraga; Canário, Luis del Sol, Alfredo di Stéfano, Ferenc Puskás, Paco Gento*
Eintracht Frankfurt: *Egon Loy; Hans-Walter Eigenbrodt, Hermann Höfer, Friedel Lutz ; Dieter Stinka, Hans Weilbächer ; Richard Kreß, Dieter Lindner, Alfred Pfaff, Erich Meier, Erwin Stein*
Referee: *Jack Mowat* (Sco)

Real Madrid had already lifted the European Cup four times in four previous seasons. Boasting of the greatest team on the planet Los Blancos had a point to prove in Glasgow, as strange as it may sound. They had lost the league to Barcelona on goal average, despite finishing level on points while cross town rivals Atletico

Madrid had dispatched them 3-1 in the Cup final. A trophy-less season with such a star studded team was almost unthinkable for Real Madrid.

Qualifying as defending champions, Real had made short work of Luxembourg champions Jeunesse Esch in first round. They lost the first leg of second round to Nice but progressed after a 4-0 win in Madrid in second leg. A crunch tie against Spanish champions Barcelona awaited in semi-final but Real's Galacticos rose to the occasion – dishing out two near perfect performances to triumph with a 3-1 score line in both legs.

Paul Oßwald won the Southern German Championship with Eintracht thrice and had coached them for a total of eight years in two separate stints between 1928 and 1938. But in his third era would Oßwald achieve his greatest success by leading the German club to their first national league title. Participating in European Cup for the first time, Eintracht qualified when their Finnish opponents Kuopion Palloseura withdrew from the competition. They defeated Swiss champions Young Boys with ease in second round before squeezing past Wiener Sports Club in a tightly contested quarter-final.

It was in the semi-final that Eintracht would play their greatest games in Europe. They were up against Scottish giants Rangers FC, who had won their domestic title three times in previous five occasions. Favourites to win the tie, Rangers manager Scot Symon landed in Frankfurt for the first leg and quipped – "Eintracht? Who are they?" An arrogance that had become a fabric of a club right up until its death in 2012. It was 1-1 at half time in Germany. The second half was a different story. Eintracht started a blitz of attacking football, scoring five times without reply. Any hope of a Rangers comeback in Glasgow were crushed by the half hour mark as Eintracht raced to a 3-1 lead, presumably with Scot Symon now realising exactly who they were. It eventually finished 6-3 to the visitors and Eintracht's 12-4 aggregate victory remains the biggest margin of win in a European Cup semi-final to date.

Ferenc Puskás had to issue a written apology to the German federation to make sure that the final took place. The German FA had banned German teams from playing a team containing Puskás after his comments following the 1954 World Cup final insinuating that West German players had doped. An international friendly had taken place in Hampden Park days before the final and teams had complained about the quality of the playing turf as well as the wind speed inside the stadium.

Eager to catch their stronger opponent's off-guard, Eintracht made a quick start and within seconds of the kick-off saw a cross from left-out Erich Meier clip Dominguez's cross-piece. Eight minutes later a long ball from Wellbacher found Kreß on the right-wing, who drifted past Pachin before rolling the ball across the goal below a diving Dominguez. Marquitos came to the rescue, putting the ball out of play as two Eintracht strikers were closing in with an open goal gaping. On the 11th minute Kreß once again got past Pachin but his little chip to set up a heading chance for Stein was blocked by Santamaria. The Germans' early adventure paid dividends three minutes after the quarter-hour mark as a clever exchange of positions saw inside-forward Linder set-up the opening goal for an unmarked Kreß.

This was precisely the wake-up call Real Madrid needed as the Galacticos took just nine minutes to find their rhythm and draw level. After a series of intricate passes Zárraga found Canário inside the box. The Brazilian dribbled past two defenders before putting in a perfect low cross between two more defenders as Di Stéfano scored a simple tap-in. Minutes later Puskás made his first productive run of the match but saw his shot being punted off the line. Unsurprisingly, Real doubled their lead on the half hour mark. A no look pass from Gento opened up a chance for Canário whose shot was weakly saved by Loy before Di Stéfano score a perfect poacher's goal.

Eintracht was getting pushed further back with Real Madrid playing their usual game but had a half chance when a cross from Kreß eluded three heads before falling for Pfaff, whose poor shot went well wide ("You can't afford to miss chances like that and still win the European Cup", quipped the BBC commentator). Six minutes before half time a sumptuous piece of play saw a half turned Del Sol release an inch perfect 40 yard long pass for Canário but the Brazilian's luck of scoring a goal certainly wasn't favouring him as his shot went wide by inches. Vidal struck the post once but Real effectively ended the game in first half itself as Puskás latched on to a loose ball inside the box before scoring with a powerful shot from a narrow angle.

Real continued to dictate proceedings in second half and created a number of chances. Puskás saw his shot saved by Loy before converting a highly contentious penalty kick on the 56th minute. Eintracht's best player in this match Kreß had a chance to cut down the lead but his shot was saved comfortably. On the 57th minute Puskás had his left-footed shot bounce off the frame-work after a lovely one-two with Di Stéfano. Wellbacher's shot met the same fate seconds later after it looped over the Real Madrid 'keeper thanks to a deflection.

Puskás doubled his tally on the hour mark by pushing in Gento's cross from the left wing after a typically powerful sprint from the winger.

The five minute spell between the 70th and 75th minutes was one of the greatest in club football history. Puskás rounded off his tally by scoring one of the best goals ever seen in a European Cup final. The Hungarian received Del Sol's pass with his back turned towards the goal, turned 180 degrees before bulging the net with his second touch. Seconds later Stein received the ball on edge of Real Madrid box, leapt and dribbled past three diving defenders before calmly looping the ball over Dominguez. 6-2.

Di Stéfano almost looked incensed by Eintracht's goal as he scored Real's seventh straight after the kick-off. Receiving the ball in midfield he began a run, swerving past a number of markers before scoring with a powerful shot from just outside the box. A minute and half later complete miscommunication between Vidal and Dominguez saw Stein score the final goal of the now legendary score-line. 7-3.

The Galacticos above all, were great showmen. As if scoring seven times was not enough, the Blancos then proceeded to show a variety of skills to entertain the capacity crowd. There was a crescendo of "ooh"s and gasps as Real came close to scoring a couple of goals more.

This proved to be the final bright spark of Real Madrid's most successful era, almost. A few months later Real Madrid would outclass a very strong Penarol side 5-0 to lift the first ever Intercontinental Cup. In the 1960/61 edition of European Cup Barcelona would become the first team to knock Real Madrid out after one of the most controversial European knock-out games ever. A year later they were back in the final but in a symbolic passing of baton, a young Portuguese striker named Eusebio would outshine Puskás and Di Stéfano as Real Madrid ended up losing 5-3. They would win one more European Cup in 1960s albeit with a completely different team and Gento as captain but neither them nor any other club would ever manage to show the same level of dominance in European Cup. Real Madrid's performance in Glasgow influenced a whole generation of coaches and players.

For Eintracht Frankfurt, their debut season in European Cup remained one of the highest points in their history. They would never really achieve anything on a similar scale and are yet to win the league title since 1959. They have won four German Cups and also achieved European success when they won the UEFA Cup Winners Cup in 1980 after beating Borussia Monchengladbach in the two legged final.

That was the official report and no mention of the referee. So, what does this have to do with the Lanarkshire Referees Association? Well, Jack Mowat (Burnside, pictured) refereed that great European Cup final in 1960 and Jack Mowat (Burnside) ran the Lanarkshire Referees Association in 1960. The acclaim given to Jack Mowat (Burnside) after this game (from inside Scotland, out of all the international newspapers that were looked at by this author, the only papers who even mentioned the referee were Scottish ones) made him a big name in Scotland and Willie Allan, then Chief Executive of the SFA, was happy to let Jack Mowat (Burnside) run refereeing in Scotland and by the time Ernie Walker took over in 1977, Jack Mowat (Burnside) had firmly entrenched the Lanarkshire Referees Association as the powerbase of refereeing in Scotland. This is important because this allowed a recruitment policy to be implemented that ensured the right kind of people got to the top of refereeing in Scotland. This was started by Jack Mowat, continued by Frank Crossley (Wishaw) and goes on through George Cumming (Carluke) today.

Jack Mowat (Burnside) went on to become the most dominant figure in Scottish refereeing for decades. He exercised a degree of control over refereeing that is normally associated with dictators like Kim Jong-un.

He appointed the Supervisors, now called Observers, in the local associations across the Country and used them to promote his views and to ensure that individual referees who progressed through the grades fitted his profile of what made a good referee and, more importantly, what type of person they were.

One of Jack Mowat's (Burnside) closest allies was Frank Crossley (Wishaw) and he was appointed as Supervisor of Lanarkshire Referees Association in 1963. Frank Crossley (Wishaw) was instrumental in identifying and grooming the key players in Lanarkshire refereeing in the last four decades – John Paterson (Bothwell), Bobby Davidson (Airdrie), Bobby Tait (East Kilbride), George Cumming (Carluke), Hugh Dallas (Bonkle), Ray Morrison (Carluke) and Don McVicar (Carluke).

Frank Crossley (Wishaw) may have been the local Supervisor but no referees were promoted without the approval of Jack Mowat (Burnside). He had the final say on the future of all referees in Scotland – if he didn't rate an up and coming referee then their career was as good as over. However, if he had a favourite then they were fast tracked to the top – George Cumming was one of those pushed through the 'system' but more of that later.

Jack Mowat (Burnside) attended meetings and functions at local Referee Associations across Scotland and was treated as a 'god' - or maybe 'supreme being' would better describe it given the company he kept – by Senior List Referees and retired refs who had been handed picked to act as Supervisors by Jack Mowat (Burnside) and his Referees Committee. He paid little or no attention to the vast majority of the referees who were there who gave up their time to officiate at boys club and amateur level.

There was little changed when Mowat passed away, the dynasty was in place with Tom 'Tiny' Wharton, another who was no friend of Celtic, taking over from his mentor and perpetuating the 'system' of promoting the 'right kind of people'.

A young ref back then would make it known he wanted to climb the ladder. This wasn't the norm for all, some guys just wanted to earn a few quid extra for beer money and nothing else, whilst others wanted to rise to the very top. So back then you'd come in, start going to classes (often in places likes community centres and church halls, the Lanarkshire Referees Association would use both in Motherwell normally) In this scenario, a Referees Observer would be sent to watch you and your performance would be assessed to see if you were of the standard required. That's the theory of course, the reality though was somewhat different.

Key figures around this time were John Paterson (Bothwell) and Bobby Davidson (Airdrie).

Both of them had retired by the late 70's but both were loathed by Celtic fans throughout the 60's and 70's. Indeed a game that Bobby Davidson (Airdrie) refereed in 1970 still rankles with all Celtic fans who saw it.

The occasion was the 1970 Scottish Cup final, Celtic versus Aberdeen and one look at the match report from that day gives you a window into what happened:

"In 28 minutes a McKay cross struck Murdoch on the upper arm at close range. Although Murdoch had his arm at his side referee Davidson gave a penalty much to Celtic's protest. Gemmell was booked for throwing the ball at the referee and Harper scored.

Four minutes later Aberdeen keeper Clark went to clear the ball from hand and only succeeded in dropping the ball at the feet of Bobby Lennox who accepted the chance and scored. The referee disallowed the goal for a foul and Johnstone was booked for protesting.

Things got worse in 38 minutes when Buchan fouled Lennox, who was in full flight, in the area. It was a sure penalty and no one knows why it was not given and the Celtic players were left enraged.

Despite a barrage of Celtic pressure Aberdeen scored on the break with 10 minutes to go. Lennox scored late on but Aberdeen clinched it with a third right after.

Celtic fans stayed at the end to berate referee Davidson but sportingly applauded Martin Buchan when he received the trophy on a cold April day.

Stein was fulsome in his praise of the Dons' performance but was scathing in his criticism of Davidson and was later to be rebuked by the SFA for his post-match comments"

This game was said to be the start of an ongoing feud between Stein and Davidson which was to go on for several years but in actual fact it started six months before. In a league game at Pittodrie. On a bitterly cold night in Aberdeen, Bobby Davidson (Airdrie) allowed an Aberdeen goal that beggared belief. After a goalmouth scramble, Celtic goalkeeper and writer of the foreword for this book, John Fallon, ran out and clutched the ball among the melee. Brian McIlroy, making his Aberdeen debut that night, ran in and kicked the ball out of Fallon's hands which allowed Joe Harper to calmly stroke the ball into an open goal. Despite huge protests from the Celtic players, the goal was allowed to stand and Stein was seething.

Celtic had a goal disallowed later in that season, versus Rangers at Celtic Park, when Billy McNeill was said by the referee to have impeded Rangers goalkeeper Gerry Neef. Observers say there was no such impediment. The referee was John Paterson (Bothwell)

Of course, despite this controversy, Bobby Davidson (Airdrie) refereed that Aberdeen cup final on April 11th 1970. His previous Celtic game? October 29th 1969 when he allowed the controversial Harper goal.

Was Bobby Davidson (Airdrie) drafted in to ensure an Aberdeen victory in that cup final?

John Paterson (Bothwell) refereed the other cup final that season, Celtic versus St. Johnstone the weekend before the game at Pittodrie, as the Lanarkshire Referees Association tightened its grip on refereeing in Scotland.

Both were very active in Lanarkshire Referees Assocation during their careers and were members of the Council. Their activity lessened as the years went on but both attended social functions for a while.

John Paterson (Bothwell) was seen as a bit of a 'snob' by others and it was said that he was type of person that was only interested in the 'top men'

Bobby Davidson (Airdrie) always wanted to be the centre of attention, that Aberdeen cup final was him in his pomp, and liked to hold court surrounded by up and coming refs who saw him as a key figure in the Lanarkshire RA.

Bobby Davidson (Airdrie) had a reputation as ladies man and it is rumoured that he suffered a heart attack in his mistress' bed after a night of heavy passion but, presumably to avoid the scandal of the affair being made public, she put him in her car and drove him to Monklands Hospital.

If you wanted to become a referee in Lanarkshire, you started refereeing boys club games and so on. The lowest level effectively. If that's all you wanted then that's all you got. If, however, you wanted to progress right to the top, then you let your superiors know and in due course observers would be sent out to watch you and start writing reports about your performances. That was the official way anyway.

If Jack Mowat (Burnside) or later Frank Crossley (Wishaw) had picked you out from the choir then that report would be written before the match had even taken place. This was certainly the case with many referees in Scotland and many observers reckon one of the main beneficiaries of this was Donald McVicar (Carluke). Widely regarded in refereeing circles as being "hopeless" his face fitted and he would climb the ladder to the point where he would be observing referees and complimenting them on giving ridiculous penalties to Rangers:

Former referee Steve Conroy is taking the Scottish FA to court for unfair dismissal. Conroy quit refereeing after being overlooked for a top flight match for three months.

His last game was the controversial game at Ibrox between Rangers and Dunfermline on 3rd December 2011. Conroy awarded Rangers a penalty after Sone Aluko was adjudged to have been fouled inside the box under a challenge from Martin Hardie.

However, an SFA fast-track tribunal subsequently banned Aluko for two matches for diving. The decision to ban the winger angered Rangers manager Ally McCoist.

McCoist, at the time, said: "The three gentlemen on the panel have effectively called my player a cheat and a liar, neither of which he is. It's an absolutely incredible decision, given that the referee is literally five yards from the incident. The panel agreed there was contact, so for them to uphold the decision and go against their own referee, who had a particularly good game, is ridiculous."

Now it seems that Conroy has been given the green light to take his case against the Scottish FA to an employment tribunal, reportedly for 'unfair dismissal and age discrimination'.

Conroy became a referee in 1993 and reached category one status in 2000. He took charge of around 300 senior games, including almost 100 in the SPL, as a category one referee.

The Ibrox match was Conroy's last SPL fixture – **a game which referee supervisor Donald McVicar, the former SFA head of referees, complimented Conroy on** *– and spent the next three months refereeing in the lower leagues.*

A date for a hearing with full details of his claims has still to be set.

Jack Mowat (Burnside), of course, was a Freemason and he had a trophy named after him, given to 'Scotland's Best Referee', which began in 1990 and the list of winners could easily be up inside a Masonic lodge. The masons who won it are denoted with, of course, an Asterisk:

1990-91	George Smith
1991-92	George Smith
1992-93	Willie Young
1993-94	Douglas Hope
1994-95	Les Mottram*
1995-96	Hugh Dallas*
1996-97	Hugh Dallas*
1997-98	Willie Young
1998-99	Hugh Dallas*
1999-00	Jim McCluskey*
2000-01	Kenny Clark
2001-02	Hugh Dallas*
2002-03	Kenny Clark
2003-04	Stuart Dougal*
2004-05	John Rowbotham
2005-06	Douglas McDonald
2006-07	Kenny Clark
2007-08	Stuart Dougal*
2008-09	Craig Thomson
2009-10	Dougie McDonald
2010-11	Calum Murray
2011-12	Craig Thomson
2012-13	William Collum
2013-14	Craig Thomson

Just Another Saturday

Refereeing has changed worldwide in the last 50-60 years and this, incredibly, applies in Scotland too. It used to be about getting ready to run out the tunnel at five to three on a Saturday afternoon or on a Wednesday night but the control major cable TV channels have on our kick-off times means that you can substitute Thursday night, Friday night, Saturday lunchtime, the variations go on and on and the demands increase year on year.

We are all used to TV and newspaper stories telling us about the way our top footballers prepare for a game, the FA Cup final coverage, for example, prides itself on this. Whisked off to a five star hotel, pampered, early to bed, early morning massage, light training session, healthy food and luxury coach trip to the stadium fully prepared for.

We even hear that some newly registered lower league clubs have tried to copy the 'big clubs' by visiting well known Golf venues like Carnoustie and Turnberry. Great idea as long as someone is carefully managing the budgets …. but that's another story.

So we know how the two teams prepare for a match but what about the other team without which there would be no match – the Referee and his Assistants.

Nobody really gives much thought to them until the first whistle blows and then their every decision is challenged and discussed by so called 'experts'. Usual conclusion likely to be that it was an 'honest mistake' and Celtic should just shut up and get on with it as it will 'even itself out over the season'.

Ok then.

A lot of fans still think that referees just throw their boots and brightly coloured Specsavers sponsored kit into a bag an hour or so before kick-off and head to the game but that's about as much reality as *Big Brother.*

So what is the match day routine of a referee heading to Celtic Park for a league match kicking off at 3pm on a Saturday? Preparing for a match does not start when the alarm goes off on a Saturday morning. Preparation takes all week before one game. Referees need to be physically fit to handle any match – from amateur, junior, Under 19 to the very top level of the game. Just like players, referees have a close season break and then do their own pre-season routine building up to the compulsory fitness test. Referees and Assistants need to pass this three times each season to stay on the list. This does create disbelief amongst fans who regularly berate officials for not keeping up with play.

Scottish referees are not full time and have jobs and fit in training early morning, lunchtime and evenings. No doubt the SFA's practice of promoting 'professional people' like Lawyers and Company Directors makes it easier for them to get away to train – not many of them are putting on the overalls and working boots to put in a shift at minimum wage with no time off and very few breaks.

Nutrition also plays a big part in a referee's preparation – again a bizarre one when you think of the likes of Willie Young lumbering up and down the park in a vain effort to get reasonably close to the play. Of course that didn't stop the likes of him and some of his colleagues being more familiar to mince pie suppers than oatmeal in the past but you can't get away with that now with preparations for games involving regular physical training and sensible eating.

The Friday night before a match would be an early dinner and quiet evening, sessions down the pub being replaced by watching a bit of TV, listening to some music and off to bed at about 11pm.

Match day starts with the alarm and it is out of bed, most Refs having a short run to loosen up the muscles for later on followed by a cold-ish shower and then a light breakfast normally including some of variation of eggs and bread.

Then it would be time to have a read at the papers – usually from the back page first to catch up on the latest football news. It is always useful for a referee to see who is injured and not playing and to look at the likely line-ups to see where the potential flashpoints are going to be – who will need to be given a quiet word in the ear early on or possibly a caution to stop the 'hammer thrower' intimidating the creative midfielder.

Grade 1 refs will say they never pre-judge a player and will all say that every game starts off with a clean slate.

If you believe that, I have some land in Florida to sell you.

Most Refs would then catch up with Sky Sports News or watch Soccer AM before it being time to pack the bag and head to the match.

The routine for matches has changed in recent years. Previously the match officials would all make their way to the Park and meet up in the Referees Room about an hour and a half before kick-off.

Well that's the official version.

The newspapers are full of expenses scandals these days involving MPs and others. Well among referees in Scotland, the same rules apply, or don't as the case normally is. Our fine upstanding brothers in refereeing in Scotland operated an expenses fiddle for as long as there have been referees getting paid to officiate in the SPFL, SPL, SFL and Scottish Cup.

Car sharing and then everyone claiming they drove to the match was widespread and accepted. A referee from, for example, Ayrshire, would pick up one Assistant in Glasgow and another at Stirling for a match in Aberdeen.

All three would claim full travelling expenses.

Another honest mistake as they just forgot that their car didn't leave the driveway.

The arrangements for officials going to Celtic Park and other grounds have changed in recent years. The officials now meet up at a local hotel for a pre-match lunch and are taken by car from there to the ground. This is arranged by the home team and has been introduced for safety reasons and to avoid match officials cars being in the car park.

Had this been in place years ago some incidents would have been avoided.

To illustrate here are a couple of examples – one amusing and one potentially dangerous.

Clubs always confirmed by postcard or letter to referees and assistants the date and time of matches. This always led to a few wry smiles when postcards arrived from Ibrox signed by one R.C. Ogilvie.

However, for a midweek match at Celtic Park the referee, Davie Syme (Rutherglen), turned up at the main door with his referee blazer and tie on and clutching his kit bag. As he went to go in the doorman, a very imposing gentleman called Bill Peacock, demanded to see his postcard confirming that he was indeed the match referee.

Syme had left the card at home.

Mr Peacock, a stickler for rules, refused him entry and he duly returned to his car in the Car Park. This was pre mobile phone so there was no way to contact anyone.

As kick-off approached there were nervous linesmen and officials wondering where the referee was. Eventually Jock Stein went searching. He asked Mr Peacock if he had seen the referee. He duly informed Big Jock what had happened and startled fans queuing to get in the match witnessed Celtic's greatest ever manager storming through the car park and telling Davie Syme (Rutherglen) to get inside and get the match started.

Obviously if Davie Syme (Rutherglen) had been brought to the front door in a club organised car this would have been avoided.

Davie Syme (Rutherglen) was notorious for some baffling decisions against Celtic. When I was writing this book I was contacted by someone called John who may shed some light as to why:

"In 1993 I was living in Germany, my eldest son was born there in February that year (the one who is going to do the web site build for you) When he was a few weeks old we arranged to drive home,

sailing from Ostend to Dover at around midnight on 3rd March 1993.

To my horror when I phoned my mate to tell him we were coming home on holiday he said I think Rangers (IL) are playing Brugge that night in Belgium. When we arrived at Ostend the port was awash with their fans. As the wife is from Dublin I informed her not to speak on the boat till we got to our cabin, never been so pleased before or since that I splashed a bit extra for something.

Anyway, we joined the queue of cars waiting to get on the ferry, we were sitting behind a car, I think it was a black Saab, as we were driving on to the ferry the occupants of the car in front were abusing the ferry staff who were guiding the cars in to place. "Ya fenian frog bastard" The fact that we were in Belgium and not France was lost on them but you have to admire them for managing to racially abuse two completely separate nations and cultures in four words! In fact make that three nations the Belgique folk were probably insulted at being confused as French!

So we end up parked on the ferry behind the same car, my car had a German plate so was happy to let the hoards assume we were German and keep our heads down. Got out the car and was assembling the pram for the baby as I observed the passenger get out the car in front, he had one of those orange scarfs proudly knotted around his neck with King Billy resplendent on his horse in full view. As I was biting my inner lip and cursing him under my breath two more came out the back of the car, more of the same. Then the driver's door opened and a rather well dressed chap in a nice suit stepped out. As he turned towards me my blood ran cold as I realised I know him, if he knows me we are in trouble.

After a a couple of seconds I realised it was none other than David Syme, at that time Grade One Scottish referee, who can forget his performance in the League Cup Final against them in 1986! I know he was still an active top flight ref in 1993 as he was the referee in the New Year game 1994 when it all kicked off at the old board.

So that is it, a guy who was touted by most of the usual suspects back then as our top whistler whose impartiality and integrity are beyond reproach, driving to a European away game with a car full of Rangers(IL) fans"

The second example happened in the early eighties at Tynecastle but had its roots at Celtic Park. In March 1983 Willie 'Bud' Johnston of Hearts was ordered off in controversial circumstances by Brian McGinlay. The controversy raged against McGinlay and his linesmen with Hearts Chairman, Wallace Mercer, making all sorts of inflammatory statements in the press.

Shortly afterwards McGinlay was officiating in a match at Tynecastle and he duly turned up to park as normal in the Tynecastle High School car park. This would normally involve a leisurely walk from there to the park.

McGinlay has told the story of that day and he was apparently met with hostility from the stewards and had to run a gauntlet of abuse from his car to the main door with Police intervening to keep fans back.

So times have changed and referees have much better protection to do more honest mistakes.

Arriving at the park kit bags would be deposited in the referee's room and it is time for a first look at the pitch - providing there was not bad weather and an earlier pitch inspection.

The referee and assistants will then have their first look at the ground conditions, which might affect which boots they wear, will check the nets and the assistants will normally have a look at the 'line' they will be running.

Back inside a quick check of team colours to make sure there are no clashes and it is back into the referee's room.

The Police Match Commander, League Delegate and Referees Observer will then join the match officials for a pre match briefing with the Police leading on safety issues and emergency signals.

Team Lines are handed in and the match is drawing closer.

Into training gear next and out onto the pitch for a warm up

Back to the referee's room and into referees kit and it is time to check the players' boots before leading out the teams and getting the match started.

Post-match it is not simply into the shower changed and off to the pub or lodge as it used to be.

Team Lines are completed with details of substitutions so to get them off to the League.

The Referees Observer will come in for a chat to clarify incidents that happened during the game. We all know about this process from the "Dougie, Dougie" incident at Tannadice.

After that it is a club car back to the hotel to collect your car.

The routine can then vary according to who the other members of the officials are that day.

If they are good friends and sociable then it will be a wind down drink at the hotel before heading home.

Again depending on which route the officials are taking on the way home there are well known pubs in all areas of the country where referees tend to meet at teatime on Saturdays after games at all levels from Amateur up to SPFL. Many a Saturday evening is spent swapping stories of that day's matches before finally arriving home.

Then the whole cycle starts again preparing for the next match.

However, in Lanarkshire, certain other procedures had to be followed too.

The Carluke Connection

The Scottish Prison Service isn't an obvious standout in terms of institutional bias. Most observers would associate any sort of "them and us" scenario in the common prison officers and prisoners divide. Yet, even in the prison service, bias was rife and used to create an outlook of Scottish society that was totally false. I spoke to two guards who both worked in HMP Barlinnie. One recalled the horror that went around his fellow guards when, attending the funeral of a former Governor, he took communion. The next shift his superior said "I didn't know you were a Catholic? You need to work in The Vatican" Assuming it was a joke, he laughed but it was revealed that there was a unit in Barlinnie that housed Catholic prisoners and was nicknamed "The Vatican". His life in the SPS was never the same again and led to a change in career. Another officer told me an astonishing story of a figures manipulation that would askew statistics for a generation. Quite simply, the officer in charge of admissions was instructed to put one word as often as possible in the box marked 'religion', that word was 'Catholic'.

Welcome to Scotland.

Carluke barely registered with me pre the Internet Bampot revolution. I would have had to try and immerse myself in the place to get a feel for it for this book were not the fact that Tic Talk and the Carluke Shamrock put Carluke on the map. So who better to talk to than Richard Swan regarding what the place, and people, are actually like?

"A large town with a village feel.

I've found that most places - with perhaps the exception of a bland and soulless "new town" like Cumbernauld or East Kilbride - have a *feeling* about them. It could be the vibrancy of Glasgow's Merchant

City area, or the historic tint found walking around St. Andrews. It might not always be a blatantly obvious trigger like the architecture, or the attire of the local inhabitants, but a definite "feel" or atmosphere to a place.

When it comes to Carluke, it's a "village" feeling that hangs over the town and also seems to colour the chat and mannerisms in the conversations between people on the streets. That village description might not be a surprise to the majority of people that have simply passed through the town, either taking the A73 north to the bigger towns of Wishaw, Motherwell, and further still to Glasgow, or taken the same road in the other direction to the likes of Lanark, Biggar, Peebles, and beyond.

However, what does surprise the visitors that actually take a tour around the town, beyond the simple in/out A73 road that slices the town in two, is the surprisingly large size of this small Clydesdale town. What started off as a tiny weaver/mining village back in the mists of time, has exploded with rail and car into a large commuting town. A railway that skirts the edge of the town takes workers in opposite directions to Glasgow and Edinburgh, and the town's position high atop the Clyde Valley, is helpfully sandwiched between both M8 and M74 major motorways.

Unlike the truly tiny villages that cluster around Carluke - like Kilncadzow, Law, Forth and the like - Carluke is on the deceptively large side, with numerous housing estates extending the town outward in all directions over the years. At one point, the national census had the place bulging just under 20,000, and it now sits at a more breathable 15,000.

However, you've really got to head off the main roads to find those secretly advancing estates to appreciate its size. If you just stick to the High Street (a highly depressing retail graveyard that was killed off with a reassigning of road traffic many years ago) or the pleasant Market Gardens (a flower garden festooned slope that bulges at the seams during the annual Gala Day) then you'd be forgiven for being tricked into thinking of it as a small village.

The other element that allows Carluke to hide its Tardis-town size, is that you can stand in the centre of town, and if you walk in absolutely any direction for only a mile or so, you'll find yourself in the countryside. Farms, woodlands, forests, reservoirs, acres of grass fields, burns, hills and slopes dropping down into the fertile Clyde Valley - all very pleasant, natural, lush, and giving the town that village feel of being coddled by a dark green blanket of nature on all sides. Unlike the Lanarkshire towns of Wishaw, Motherwell, Hamilton and so on, which blend and merge into each other's concrete with barely a border between them, Carluke has very much a feeling of being cut-off and separate from surrounding areas. That separation is something that's very apparent during bad winters where exit roads are easily closed off, leaving the town feeling like a lone, Arctic outpost.

That village feel of smallness and the belief that "everyone knows everyone" also probably stems from the historic nature of the town, which makes it feel like a place where time has stood still, although the invasion of modern behemoths like Tesco superstores try to fight that history.

The "Grandfather of the Ordnance Survey" maps - Major General William Roy - has his birthplace celebrated with a local monument on one of the many woodland edges of the town. A distinguished geologist and palaeontologist - Dr Daniel Rankin - has his many discoveries and research celebrated by town plaques and stained glass window motifs. And such a small town also boasts of not one, not two, but three Victoria Cross holders from the 1st World War - one of them being William Angus, born in 1888 and recorded as a player in the books of Celtic Football Club.

With the historical past of weaver industry cottages and coal mines long gone, the mainly "commuter" residency of the town leaves a bare minimum of industry on show. Ramsay of Carluke - the wold famous butchers and bacon curers, cited and recommended by the likes of Rick Stein and Heston Blumenthal - occupy a large part of the real estate and focus in town. Although the even larger Scott's Jamworks and chocolate factory holds more prominence in the town's skyline, and also being the home of the "Carluke Steak" - also known as: "a piece and jam!"

A high school, more than half a dozen primary schools, and several nurseries give the town's demographics an energetic quotient of kids - especially seen during Gala Day when a long line of floats are paraded through the town, having been decorated and presented by each school and kids' club. However, it is the rather sad and burgeoning list of pubs, bookies and takeaway places that lends the town a more sombre and depressing "working class Scotland" image.

That working class personality of course bleeds into the town's population of football supporters. Like pretty much every Lanarkshire place, with the notable exceptions of the likes of Coatbridge, Carluke has always had a blue majority. You can count on one hand the number of Hearts or Aberdeen fans in the town, and you can start to fill a bus with those who frequent Fir Park (if they were ever organised to actually have a bus; not seen since their 1991 cup final), but it's very much a blue majority that has always previously dominated the town. A background that makes the birth and expansion of the local Carluke Shamrock C.S.C. into the dominant position of most prominent, vocal, organised and well run football supporters club all the more admirable.

Since their Glasgow club died an embarrassing and painful death in 2012, that blue majority has become much less vocal, much less visible, and much less supportive of football events, but it is still very much there, lurking and lying low in the town's shadows. It can be spotted by patient observers every year during summer, when the lesser spotted bluenose can be seen to venture into the sunlight and enjoy the cultural expression of flute bands bussed in from other areas around the country, usually feasting on a deep-fried diet causing massive waist expansion, and the consumption of a tonic wine that leads to poor motor skills, vastly reduced communication prowess, and sometimes complete bladder malfunction. Bless.

The hooped contingent of the town - the #shambolic crew of the Carluke Shamrock C.S.C. - were united together as a cohesive band of brothers when a rare Lanark/Carluke agreement found the club formed in 1987. The very first outing - a dreary 4-1 defeat to Dundee away at Dens - was probably the perfect expression of the C.S.C. at that time. It personified the struggle and the pain felt during those hard times supporting Celtic during "The Asterisk Years", and also for the C.S.C. building itself up against a very hostile atmosphere. Although Carluke has never held a blatantly sectarian agenda like the infamy of Larkhall, nor does it contain a tangible construction like the Orange Order halls of Wishaw and

Motherwell, that blue majority although perhaps more silent (or sneakier?) still held sway in the town for a long time, and made its presence obvious to any resident daring to wear the famous green and white hoops in public.

The existence of the refereeing fraternity in and around town was always well known and often discussed amongst the football supporting population, but again that presence was also not blatant, and also kept to the same hushed and protected whispered tones of the silent majority. Celtic fans in the town could throw their arms in the air at every blatant "honest mistake" they would witness on match day, or they could point to known or suspected connections through families and friends that seemed to link these all powerful whistlers, but not much could be done besides that. This was a fully sanctioned, approved, accepted, and rubber stamped fraternity that was protected by authorities and media alike. Besides....we were just paranoid"

Lanarkshire were always one of the more influential associations in Scottish refereeing, along with Glasgow and Ayrshire, with Renfrew, Edinburgh, Tayside and Stirling less influential. LRA supervisor Frank Crossley (Wishaw) was close to Jack Mowat (Burnside) who was the real power broker through the 70's and 80's so the LRA influence grew. To the point where the Lanarkshire Referees Association has controlled refereeing in Scotland now for over 50 years as power passed to Frank Crossley (Wishaw) and then to George Cumming (Carluke).

Like any institution with a "if your face fits" mentality the cream doesn't always rise to the top.

Mike Delaney (Cleland) joined the Senior List in 1970 and became a Class 1 referee in 1976. He served at that category for 12 seasons. He was appointed a Referee Supervisor for SFA Referees' (Lanarkshire) in 1990 and served in that capacity until 2005 when the structure changed to the separate roles of Association Manager and Referee Observer. Mike Delaney (Cleland) was very much a yes man. A staunch Catholic, he did what he was told by the likes of Frank Crossley (Carluke).

He shot to fame in 1986 when he refereed Graeme Souness' first official appearance in a Rangers jersey. And sent him off. Now critics of this book will jump on that, they will say, and I am paraphrasing here, "Oh aye, so they all want to Celtic to get beat but they send Souness off?" and it's a valid point or at least would be if the context told us something completely different.

You see Mike Delaney (Cleland) had an awful game that day and had no choice but to send off Souness. He had already booked him for a brutal assault on Billy Kirkwood in full view of everyone, a tackle very similar to the one he would go on to commit on Billy Stark a year later, and a tackle that would see the player shown a red card immediately these days. So when Souness went onto to lash out at George McCluskey, again, in full view of everyone, Mike Delaney (Cleland) had no choice but to send him off. However it was the other decisions that Mike Delaney (Cleland) made that day that tell the real story. Hibs went 1-0 up in the game, through new signing Stuart Beedie, and were well in control when Ally McCoist did a dive in the box so good that the Hibernian fanzines would refer to him from then on in as "Greg Louganis" and stayed down as if poleaxed. I say a good dive but watching it again gives you no other feeling than to cringe. Yet Mike Delaney (Cleland), a full 30 yards behind the play, gave Rangers a penalty instantly much to the chagrin of Alan Rough and the rest of the Hibs defence. McCoist made a remarkable recovery to take and score the penalty to make the score 1-1.

Then came the Souness red card.

Now, just after Souness lashes out at George McCluskey, Rangers striker Colin West punches Hibs defender Mark Fulton in the face. Mike Delaney (Cleland) is four yards from the incident yet only books West.

Hibs go 2-1 up before half time through Steve Cowan but this would not be Cowan's last significant contribution in the game. Chasing a loose ball in the second half, at the Cowshed end, Cowan tugs at the shirt of Terry Butcher much in the same way a child would playing tig in the playground. Butcher then lashes out with an elbow in the face of Cowan much in the same way Conor McGregor would in the MMA. After the usual fracas that follows such incidents, Mike Delaney (Cleland) books both players. So pulling a shirt is the same as elbowing in the face? As much as a penalty a yard outside the box is the same as a handball that stops a treble.

And what of George McCluskey, the main victim of the thug behaviour from Souness. When I mentioned the incident to him a wry smile went on his face and he said "He was trying to take out the hard man wasn't he?"

*

Frank Crossley was born in Yorkshire and would have got on famously with a more recent arrival from a part of the world better known for Last of the Summer Wine and Emmerdale than connections to Scottish football.

A bluff, blunt speaking Yorkshireman with little or no sense of humour who didn't pay a penny to watch football in Scotland but made a few bob out of it. Frank Crossley or Charles Green – take your pick because the description fits both.

Following the example of his friend and leader Mowat, Crossley like the other hand picked Supervisors in other areas, paid little or no attention to amateur or junior referees until his trusted lieutenants – better known as the Association's Council – identified candidates for the Senior List.

Invariably these would be from the right background – teachers, lawyers and other professions – who fitted the 'profile' that could be moulded into an SFA Referee.

If they already attended the right meetings out with refereeing so much the better. If not they were encouraged to join because it would help their careers to be seen mixing in the right company.

Crossley kept all but a small number at arm's length and we are told that he simply handed Referees' reports on their performance with little or no comment – unless it was one of his 'band of brothers' who would then be given as much time and advice as they needed.

Our source tells us that he and fellow refs from other Associations would groan when they spotted 'Old Crossley' at their matches, knowing that with his links to Mowat, a poor performance could be the beginning of the end of their hopes of promotion to a higher Grade, or that Crossley had been hand-picked by Mowat to give a report which would make or break their ambitions to move up the refereeing ladder.

Crossley did not socialise with his referees, avoiding social events other than those he was obliged to attend – although he did have had many sociable nights at 'secret' meetings across Lanarkshire.

George Cumming (Carluke, pictured)

In his refereeing career George Cumming (Carluke) never made the FIFA list, never handled a European Cup tie, wasn't given an international match, didn't do Celtic v Rangers and didn't get awarded as much as a semi-final tie in Scotland never mind a final.

GEORGE CUMMING might not be a name many associate with the pinnacle of world football – but that's exactly where the Lanarkshire man ended up.

The 63-year-old took the giant leap from centre-half with Hamilton Accies, Partick Thistle and St Mirren to becoming a Grade One official in Scotland. He joined the Scottish Football Association (SFA) then the Federation of International Football Associations (FIFA), the sport's worldwide governing body, as referee supervisor.

George has spent the last two years in Kuala Lumpur, where he was the referee supremo with the Asian Football Confederation (AFC) and head of their innovative Project Future. It puts the cream of the continent's young referees through an intense two-year programme aimed at providing officials for major events such as World Cups and Asian Cups.

Although back living in Hamilton, George remains a consultant to the AFC and still regularly travels long distances to attend courses.

Former Dalziel High pupil George explained how it all started, saying: "I was a professional player then went to Carluke and I was player-coach up there for a wee while.

"I drifted away from the game for a bit but then I wanted to do something to get a bit of exercise and went to the Lanarkshire referee classes in Motherwell.

"I started refereeing in the Lanarkshire amateur league, did fairly well, got promoted and eventually got on to the Scottish Grade One list.

"I was Grade One for three years while I was the deputy-head of Lesmahagow High School. One day, I got a phone call from Ernie Walker, who was SFA secretary at the time, to ask if I would go in to have a chat with him. They were going to appoint somebody to be their referee training officer and they wanted me to do it.

"I had to think it over because I had been teaching for over 20 years and I had a high position in the school – but I thought I would give it a go.

"That was 1987 or 88, so I left teaching, went to the SFA, and I've been involved in football now for the last 20-odd years. It has given me a nice life."

Former Motherwell resident George added: "I was in charge of refereeing in Scotland for 13 years. I started off as referee training officer, then it was referee development director, and I then got a call from FIFA to ask if I would go and be their first head of refereeing.

"I lived in Zurich for two years and I was in charge of referees at the 2000 Olympic Games and 2002 World Cup.

"I decided to leave FIFA at the end of 2002, to come back home, but I still acted as a consultant.

"Then I got a call two-and-a-half years ago from Asia to ask if I was interested in going across there to help with their development work for young referees.

"I was over in Kuala Lumpur for two years, in charge of their young referee development programme.

"Some of the referees I have trained were in charge of games at the recent World Cup, and they did very well."

George admitted that having been a player helped him as a referee, but insists that everything changes as soon as you pick up the whistle.

He said: "Playing is the best part of football – I loved my time and I played at a fairly high level – but when I was refereeing, I enjoyed that as well.

"I'm on a different side of things because it's all about the administration of referees and it's very interesting to see young officials coming through."

"Being a footballer has helped in refereeing because you get a feel for the game. You can relate to the players."

"But the minute you step over the line from being a footballer to being a referee, you're a decision-maker, a law man, and not everybody is going to agree with what you say."

"You can relate to them, they can relate to you. At the end of the day, I was refereeing players that I had played alongside and managers who were had been players in my day.

"You've got a professional relationship with them. You go out there and call things as you see them, and when you've got to take action, you've just got to do it."

"The best referees are the ones who make the least mistakes. If you don't notice the referee, it means he has had a good game."

George has no doubt that he has been very fortunate to have had globe-trotting top jobs in football, and is grateful for the opportunities.

He said: "I've enjoyed it. Football has given me a great life and I've been very lucky to have been at the top level."

George Cumming was guaranteed rapid promotion through the ranks of Scottish Referees from the moment he attended his first Referee class at Motherwell YMCA.

Why? What singled him out from the other aspiring referees?

Because he ticked a number of boxes for Mowat and Co. – an ex footballer who could become a grade one Referee. Being a teacher, living in Carluke and in the same secret society as McVicar and Morrison were merely bonus balls.

The debate about referees not having a 'feel' for the game and not having played at the top flight had resurfaced as it did from time to time. Some wanted ex-pros to be put straight into the top tier of refereeing. Mowat and his men had staunchly resisted but the pressure was building on them for probably the only time in their lives.

With that being said, Cumming was manna from heaven for them. Someone who had played at senior level and who was young enough to go through the various levels to get to the top.

But Cumming was fast tracked from day one. He spent the minimum time at each grade before moving up the ladder.

Referees in other Associations who had put in the time and effort at the lower leagues were pissed off but not surprised at Mowat and Crossley pushing their ex-pro up the ladder at their expense.

Hand-picked Supervisors from Mowat's team were sent to give Cummings top marks to push him up the rankings. Regardless of his performance.

Then, surprise, surprise, early in his spell as a Grade 3a Linesman – that is what they used to call Assistant Referees- he was running the line at Rugby Park in a Kilmarnock versus, yes you've guessed it, Rangers (IL) match in the early 80s.

TV cameras were there and then the Referee gets 'injured'. The Linesman – Cumming- has to take over as Referee for a Premier Division game.

Was it just fate or was the referee injury feigned to give Cumming a high profile break which led to his promotion to Grade One the next season?

Make your own mind up but I don't believe in coincidences where the SFA Referees and funny handshakes are concerned.

An undistinguished career as a Referee then saw him hand-picked by Ernie Walker, no doubt with Mowat and Crossley in the background, to become the first Referee Development Officer when there were a host of better qualified candidates with more experience available.

George Cumming would have received a warm handshake to welcome him to the SFA hierarchy.

Cumming set about revamping referee training and development using his teaching background. As a result, experienced, professional men were treated like schoolchildren and lectured on everything from fitness to how to talk to players and club officials. Discretion and ability to man manage were replaced by 'doing it by the book'. The long slippery slope to today's poor bunch of robot referees began with Cumming's appointment.

He then established the Lanarkshire / Carluke dynasty by rewarding his friend, Brother McVicar, with a cushy job as his deputy with the line of succession clearly established. Hugh Dallas would follow on from McVicar – with disastrous consequences for Hugh, eventually.

Donald McVicar (Carluke, pictured) once remarked "I'm a bigger hero at Ibrox than Barry Ferguson"

McVicar was not a popular figure among referees out with Lanarkshire, in fact I understand that even in his local Association he was not particularly well liked.

A snobbish, pompous man he looked down his nose at those who were not of a 'professional' background and kept very much within the Carluke clique and their hangers-on.

McVicar was a very average referee, many fans would have looked at the match programme and had that sinking feeling on reading 'Referee – D.McVicar (Carluke)'.

Why? Quite simply they knew they were in for a match peppered with poor decisions, controversy and potentially yet another 'honest mistake'.

When McVicar was in his final season a Grade 2 he was having what could at best be described as an average season and, at worst, a shocker. Most observers of Scottish refereeing, and if truth be told, most referees, expected McVicar to be demoted to Grade 3b (Linesman).

That is when the Crossley / Mowat connection went into operation.

Hand-picked Supervisors boosted his marks and pushed him up the Grade Two rankings and ensured his promotion to Grade One the following season.

As his refereeing career drew to a close many people in refereeing, and no doubt at clubs across the country, breathed a sigh of relief that they were seeing the back of a poor referee.

How wrong they were.

Once again, the Brothers moved in and the Carluke Connection would kick in and McVicar's reward for being a poor referee is a place in the SFA's Refereeing Section as Cumming's deputy.

So here we had it, two men, neither of whom was a particularly good referee, were now dictating how refereeing in Scotland would be developed and, more importantly, who they wanted to see promoted to the top of the tree in refereeing in Scotland. Is it any wonder standards have plummeted over the last 25 years?

*

Ray Morrison (Carluke) was a lover of red wine and good looking women.

Morrison's early career as a referee gave no hint of the senior position he would ultimately hold within the Lanarkshire Association and within the SFA's refereeing hierarchy.

He made steady, if unspectacular, progress through the lower reaches of refereeing and was always known as 'one of the lads' who enjoyed a good night out. He did not initially appear to be one of the 'establishment' in Lanarkshire.

He was a reasonably good referee but his sneering facial expressions and dismissive treatment of players put him very firmly in the McVicar mould of looking down at people he considered to be beneath him.

Always a fitness fanatic, he was very image conscious regarding his appearance and expensive clothes.

Each area of the country had favourite pubs where it was well known that you would find referees 'socialising' after matches on a Saturday. Our source tells us that if you were in Glasgow, the Alhambra was the place to go, and in Edinburgh the Centurion in Corstorphine was always guaranteed to have a fair number of referees till late evening. In Lanarkshire the Windmill Tavern in Uddingston was a favourite haunt of Morrison and a few others.

However, after Cumming was appointed by the SFA, Morrison became a reformed character and joined the establishment and he would go back to his home town of Carluke (Not Carluke surely...) after games.

He became a close ally of Cumming, McVicar and Hugh Dallas – setting himself up to take over as the SFA's main man in Lanarkshire. This opened doors to SFA appointments and his name regularly featured on Disciplinary Panels dealing with players and managers – notably Neil Lennon.

Incidentally, for all his reputation as a ladies man, he was married. Indeed his wife was well known, particularly at the golf club. Whose badge looks vaguely similar to...

At Our Expense

Whistler's call is off-side

CELTIC fans will be outraged that former ref Brian McGinlay referred to them as "fenian b******s" at a RANGERS dinner.

He was speaking at Ian Durrant's testimonial dinner and joked: "I refereed many Old Firm games – and I made sure those fenian b******s never won any!"

The ex-whistler shocked guests by repeatedly using the term "fenian".

One guest said: "McGinlay thought he was being funny but he's just fuelling hatred and undermining Rangers' success."

The comments will disgust fellow referees who have been the target of Celtic fans' conspiracy theories.

Brian McGinlay said: "There's no bias in Scottish football.

"This was lighthearted and doctored to suit the audience."

In 2009 more than half the Commons was ordered to repay a total of £1.1million to the taxpayer - though astonishingly, dozens of MPs had failed to cough up even as an official audit was made public.
To compound their shame, it emerged that MPs enjoyed a final year on the gravy train as scandal was brewing, upping their claims yet again.

MPs claimed a record £95.6million between them in expenses in 2008-09, an increase on £92.9million the year before.

And despite the sum MPs have been ordered to repay, it became clear the taxpayer is the biggest loser in the expenses scandal, as the bill for the Legg inquiry ran to a total of £1.16million.
Today, in the culmination of the expenses scandal that has convulsed Parliament for almost a year, police gave the go-ahead to bring criminal charges against three MPs and one peer.

The Crown Prosecution Service considered police evidence files on a total of six MPs and peers.
The MPs involved are former minister and MP for Scunthorpe Elliott Morley, Bury North MP David Chaytor and Livingston's Jim Devine, while also charged is Conservative peer Lord Hanningfield, who is leader of Essex County Council.
Announcing the charges under the Theft Act, Keir Starmer said that one further case was still being investigated, while there was insufficient evidence to bring charges against Labour peer Lord Clarke of Hampstead

Files on six parliamentarians accused of the worst excesses in the second homes expenses scandal were passed by police to the Crown Prosecution Service in November and December.
The decision on criminal charges comes after Parliament endured its darkest day yesterday as grasping MPs faced judgment over the expenses scandal and the prospect of criminal charges loomed. More than half the Commons was ordered to repay a total of £1.1million to the taxpayer - though astonishingly, dozens of MPs had failed to cough up even as an official audit was made public.

To compound their shame, it emerged that MPs enjoyed a final year on the gravy train as scandal was brewing, upping their claims yet again. MPs claimed a record £95.6million between them in expenses in 2008-09, an increase on £92.9million the year before.

Sir Thomas Legg, the auditor brought in to trawl through four years of claims, yesterday delivered a devastating verdict as he concluded that 389 of 752 current and former MPs had wrongly claimed money from the taxpayer.

He condemned a 'culture of deference' that meant MPs' claims were rarely challenged and dismissed the excuse that they had been allowed by the Commons fees office.
He pointed out that all MPs had to abide by a code of conduct that required ' selflessness, accountability, honesty and leadership'.

Taxpayer-funded allowances, Sir Thomas said, should never have been used as a 'supplementary source of income'.

Despite having had weeks to pay up, it emerged that a total of 76 MPs still owed money as his report was published - and several former MPs who owe the taxpayer thousands of pounds had simply failed to respond at all.

The report said only around £800,000 of what is due had been returned to the public purse, amid speculation that some MPs may simply refuse to pay up.

According to yesterday's report, those with sums outstanding include Tory MP David Heathcoat-Amory, who has been told to hand back £23,569.69; Sir Peter Viggers, whose claims for a duck house came to symbolise the scandal, who owes £13,245.80; immigration minister Phil Woolas, who has been asked for £886.16; and LibDem frontbencher Don Foster, who owes £4,275.74.

This has led to the public having an almost total mistrust of politicians.

From the SFA:
Expenses

A 45p per mile rate is payable for travel expenses where a car is used. This payment is to be made to the driver of the car only – no expenses will be paid in respect of any fellow official travelling as a passenger.

Claims should be based on the point of departure for the match appointment i.e. home or work place as applicable – to the end point of the journey.

For match officials who travel by either train or bus, the standard fare as incurred will be reimbursed (for whole or part of journey, as applicable) on the submission of a receipt.

Match officials who travel independently to an agreed meeting point and then travel with another official by car to the match are entitled to submit a claim for such separate parts of their journey (to and from the match) as applicable.

It's hard to put a figure on how much referees in Scotland have defrauded Scottish football but there are many aspects to their general attitude regarding taking more money than they are due that make them prime targets for corruption and top European clubs knew this.

There had already been a scandal involving a Scottish referee in Europe. JPR Gordon (Newport on Tay) was caught taking designer suits from Juventus and AC Milan on different occasions in return for giving favourable refereeing decisions. It was widely known in refereeing circles that Gordon used to take an empty suitcase to refereeing assignments in Europe knowing full well that the same suitcase would be coming back full of designer clothes and gifts from the club he found favour with.

Gordon had been known in refereeing circles for decades and was refereeing from an early age, no matter the circumstances as Andy Walker from Lochee remembers:

"A game took place in season 1963/64 on Lochee Park.

I had just finished playing for my school team and, as you did in those times, we were changing behind the goal.

Our sports teacher Eric Sadler, who was a qualified Scottish referee, said he was going to speak to his two colleagues before they started their game on an adjacent pitch.

His two fellow-referees in charge of this other game were JPR Gordon, of Newport on Tay, and Bert Crocket from Dundee.

They were officiating at the U/15 Scottish Cup semi-final between the Dundee Deaf and Dumb select side and their Edinburgh counterparts.

Each referee took a half, with each team official running their line.

As in our football today, the flag was raised for all to see that a throw-in, corner, &c, was being awarded but, during play, instead of using a whistle, the referees waved white hankies for the action to halt.

All decisions were accepted and, to be honest, there were some meaty tackles.

However, any contentious behaviour immediately ceased with the waving of the hankies"

It was also widely known among clubs in Europe that Scottish referees could be 'bought', designer suits heading to the East Coast summed it up.

That doesn't mean that all Scottish referees were on the fiddle, but most in the 60's, 70's and 80's were.

Three Scottish officials got a gig for a top club's UEFA cup tie in the 1980's.

One, a famous Scottish referee, instructed his two linesman to leave their cars at home and he would pick them up. The expenses claim showed three different journeys obviously.

The referee also told his linesmen he would book their flights, from Glasgow, via another European city, then onto where they would be officiating.

Even before they had left Scotland, the expenses claim was already false but that was as much a part of the referee make up as cards and a whistle.

Upon arriving in the city they were officiating in, the lunchtime on the day before the game, they were picked up at the airport by two officials from the home club and taken to a luxury five star hotel in the middle of the city.

They were explicitly told to order what they liked from room service. One of the Scots remarked "Fuck me, the bedroom here is bigger than ma hoose"

In these days, the officials were entirely the responsibility of the home team in a European match.

After a few hours sleep on beds plusher than a carpet from John Lewis, they were picked up again by the same two officials and taken on a tour of the city. From there they were told there were reservations at the finest steakhouse in town and to order what they liked, the club were footing the bill.

After a few glasses of Pinot Noir to wash down their prime rib, the Scots went to bed on their fine Egyptian cotton and got a good night's sleep.

The next day, after a continental breakfast, they were taken to ground and given the grand tour including the trophy room and museum with photos of famous players past and present.

From there, it was off for a four course lunch, no alcohol with it being game day and then a trip back to the hotel for a few more hours sleep, albeit with a detour to a department store that was remarked upon by the Scots that was "Like fucking Grace Brothers" and they were told to each get a gift that the club would pay for.

The referee among the three Scots instructed his two linesman to "Only get something that will fit in your suitcase"

Why did he say that?

Well, these officials, despite partaking in the car fiddle like all referees and linesman, were not really corrupt. You see, none of them were in a certain Referees Association and weren't raised in a climate of corruption.

So when the game took place and the home side lost on the away goals rule, the home team officials were angry.

At full time the two chaperones burst into the referee's room, expressions on their faces akin to a wife walking in on a cheating husband at it, and screaming expletives in their native tongue.

As the three Scots looked up in astonishment, one of the home team officials said "We thought we had done enough over the last two days to guarantee the result. We have never had this problem before with Scots"

The Scots officials made their own way to the airport.

The key point is, if a few suits and designer gifts could sway them, what sort of actions would their own prejudices fuel?

When Jim Was Foiled By Albert

In Scotland, any association with Celtic or any time Celtic are associated with something, can mean a target can go on your back. This can be in something trivial, like a slagging, or it can be something hugely important, like trying to fix a football match. A slagging is something we all get somewhere along the line and certain phrases come flying out the mouths of people quicker Ballyregan Bob out of a trap.

We all know the most common one.

St Johnstone were playing Brechin at Glebe Park in 2003. After a tackle, ex Celtic player Simon Donnelly was called a 'Fenian Bastard' by Brechin City player Kevin Fotheringham. The irony wasn't lost on Donnelly, son of an ex Rangers player. The die was cast for Fotheringham though, you played for Celtic, then you're a Fenian bastard in my eyes.

By the way, Kevin Fotheringham does sound a lovely chap.

East Fife midfielder Kevin Fotheringham has received an eight-match ban following accusations he racially abused Stranraer's Gregory Tade.

The 32-year-old's club have appealed against the ban, which follows an incident involving French midfielder Tade on 2 January.

The SFA said Fotheringham had been found guilty of unacceptable conduct during the Third Division match.

East Fife said the club would "continue to support our player 100%".

In a statement, the SFA said: "Kevin Fotheringham was found guilty of unacceptable conduct as a consequence of remarks made towards player Gregory Tade and an eight-match ban was imposed."

Fotheringham was accompanied by East Fife chief executive Sid Collumbine and team-mate Paul Stewart at the hearing.

The appeal will be heard by the disciplinary appeals tribunal and the ban is therefore set aside pending the outcome of the hearing.

A date has yet to be set for the hearing.

Simon Donnelly could brush that off, there are things though that are a little harder to cope with.

Oh and Kevin Fotheringham? He continues to be employed in Scottish football.

When someone reaches the top of the tree within the Governing Body of a national sport you almost take it for granted that they are steeped in the tradition of their chosen sport. You expect them to have either competed in the sport at a reasonably high level or, at the very least, have been a fan of the sport and have been appointed to high office due to a combination of their love for and knowledge of the sport combined with other talents in finance, governance or other key aspects of running a national sporting institution.

When the Scottish Football League and then The Scottish Football Association appointed Jim Farry as their most senior paid official the above identikit wasn't even thought of. Farry's 'football career' started as clerk in the SFA's offices in Glasgow. He was an excellent administrator and was quickly promoted through the ranks and, after Willie Allen left the Scottish League, Farry became their youngest ever Secretary in the late 70s.

One of the things that caused major problems in the building industry in the past was the belief that the best joiner or brickie should be promoted to Foreman. Didn't matter that they had no managerial or financial skills, if you could build the best brick wall you got promoted.

It isn't too big a leap to see the similarities with Farry's appointments at the League and SFA.
The best administrator got to be The Secretary. Farry's problem wasn't that he couldn't manage an organisation – this was a man who was meticulous about everything to do with the SFA right down to how many paper clips were in the cupboard and could quote the Rule book verbatim without taking time out to check if he was right – he invariably was.

His big problem was that he wasn't "a Football Man"

Farry's great sporting love was Rugby. He was never happier than when chasing a funny shaped ball around a pitch or mixing with the rugby crowd at Cambuslang or Murrayfield. He had no real interest in football other than to collect his salary every month whilst working in it. As a result he didn't have a 'feel for the game' and was never comfortable mixing with football people. Farry was far more at ease with the Rugby crowd and always looked down his nose on those who paid to watch football in Scotland.

He would claim credit for the redevelopment of Hampden, but not once had he ever stood behind the goals at either the King's Park end or the Mount Florida end trying to see the action on the pitch. This was despite his Rugby friends having the right idea – demolish the rundown Murrayfield and completely rebuild it. While Jim and his Cambuslang Rugby Club mates enjoyed their Six Nations matches in the comfort of a modern stadium the Tartan Army, and those attended semi-finals and finals at Hampden, had to march along to the third rate national stadium.

His predecessor at the SFA was always comfortable talking football with International superstars, junior footballers or even referees whereas Farry stayed aloof. At the League contact with referees was down to Maureen Cooper – and if you failed this version of "The Cooper Test" your career was as good as over. More of this later.

Employees of the SFA, referees or otherwise, only got to meet Farry on very rare occasions and he always seemed distant and disinterested to them when they did meet him. It appeared on the surface that he was looking down on people, which is true, but it was also that he had no real interest in football people and very little in common with them. Farry avoided going to events like Referee Association dinners and monthly meetings but was always careful to ensure the SFA were represented – just not very often by him.

You cannot criticise his ability as an administrator, organiser and expert on rules and constitutions. His office looked as if it was inhabited by someone with OCD – a place for everything and everything in its place. It was remarked that he was very similar to the *Martin Bryce* character, played by Richard Briers, in the popular 80's sit-com *Ever Decreasing Circles*.

This passion for rules and organisation make the infamous Jorge Cadete affair even more of a mystery. Unless some mysterious secret influences were at work it is difficult to reconcile for anyone who knew Jim Farry the administrator with that man who lost his job by delaying Cadete's transfer.

No one believes he could have simply made a mistake.

Not least the panel who found him guilty of deliberately withholding Jorge Cadete's transfer so that he could not play in match for Celtic against Rangers. It would be easy to say that Farry was simply pro-Rangers but no one who knew Farry ever saw any bias towards Rangers. Indeed the newspaper report at the time fails to shed any light on the reasons for Farry's actions:

Celtic win Farry fight
David McKinney
Tuesday, 2 March 1999
(Independent)

JIM FARRY'S football career is effectively at an end after the Scottish Football Association chief executive was yesterday suspended over the Jorge Cadete affair. Celtic have claimed for three years that Farry delayed the processing of the transfer of the Portuguese player in time for the Scottish Cup semi-final against Rangers in 1996. Celtic lost the game 2-1, but yesterday they won the war against the most powerful figure in the Scottish game.

105

The SFA has offered Celtic a written apology as well as agreeing to pay compensation and meet Celtic's legal fees, and Fergus McCann, the Celtic chief executive, yesterday wasted little time in condemning the part played by Farry. "It has taken Celtic and its supporters three years to receive justice on the issue of the SFA's chief executive Jim Farry's failure to properly register Jorge Cadete.

"It is deplorable that a prominent member club should be disadvantaged in this way when on several occasions the SFA's chief executive had the opportunity to make the correct decision. Mr Farry's failure to properly and timeously register Jorge Cadete leaves the club in no other position than to ask for the office bearers of the SFA to recognise that Mr Farry's position is untenable. This case demonstrates clearly that Mr Farry cannot be allowed to hold and exercise such powerful authority."

The issue recently went to arbitration with the SFA admitting liability before proceedings could finish. Clearly angered by the whole situation, Celtic are demanding the dismissal of Farry, who has held the top job at the SFA since 1990 following 10 years as secretary of the Scottish League.

In the last nine years he has been frequently criticised for his dictatorial attitude which at times appeared out of tune with the ordinary supporter. He insisted on Scotland playing a European Championship qualifier on the day of the funeral of Princess Diana only to back down in the face of severe pressure and criticism.

Farry's motives for delaying the Cadete transfer remain unclear and although Celtic supporters will interpret his actions as indicating a pro-Rangers stance McCann refused to be drawn on the topic. "I'm not claiming there was malice but there was intent. There was a failure on his part despite the advice of Fifa and Celtic. This is a matter that goes beyond Celtic Football Club, it's a question of somebody who has failed to follow the rules of football."

McCann intends to hold discussions with the other clubs in the Scottish Premier League and his frustration with the powerbrokers at the SFA could prove the motive towards a shift of power towards the new body who would effectively run the elite body of Scottish football. In the meantime Farry has agreed to co-operate with an SFA investigation into his actions.

No evidence has ever came to light of Jim Farry being pro-Rangers. There is evidence of him being anti-Celtic though.

It's a widely held belief in Scotland that a referee, upon reaching his retirement, can pick whom he wants to referee in his last game.

While this certainly did happen it doesn't tell the whole story because it suggests that they cannot do that at any other time. Passing the "Maureen Cooper Test" allowed them to do whatever they wanted. And plenty took advantage.

It is also important to remember at this point that it is a fairly recent innovation that referees would only know a week before a game where they would be refereeing at the weekend. It is important to know that this was not the case in the 80's because referees would know 2-3 months in advance where they would be refereeing and with who, so they could make travel plans and arrangements accordingly.

Referees and Linesmen received an A4 envelope through the post containing the 'Ballot' . This showed all matches, including reserve games, for a period of 2/3 months and every Referee could see not only their own games but also who had been appointed to all other games.

So let's clarify this. In spring 1986 everyone at the SFA, and all refereeing associations that are part of it, knew who would be refereeing the last game of the 1985/86 season at Dens Park between Dundee and Hearts. It wasn't going to be the lifelong Hearts supporter, Bill Crombie (Edinburgh). Yet it was Bill Crombie who refereed the game. It was Bill Crombie who received a phone call three days previous to the game saying he would now be refereeing it. Something that rarely, if ever, happened. So why did he referee the game and who was it that called him?

It was widely known in refereeing circles that Bill Crombie was a diehard Hearts supporter. Born and raised in Edinburgh, he was a regular visitor to Tynecastle and was one of two well-known Jambos at the top level of refereeing in Scotland (The other being George Smith). When he got the call a few days before the game at Dens Park it is certain that Bill Crombie had no idea what had been happening behind the scenes that week. Bill Crombie wasn't a member of the Lanarkshire Referees Association nor did he have the mind-set required. Bill was popular among referees without being one of the main men. He was never considered one of the best referees despite his long career but he was seen as fair, honest and a good guy to have a pint with, often in The Centurion in

Corstorphine, Edinburgh, which was the post-match haunt of referees from Edinburgh or who had refereed in Edinburgh that day. So Bill Crombie was put in an unenviable position. He knew what the perception was from everyone about his Hearts loyalties and he knew he would have to be 100% fair in the game. This wasn't a problem for Bill Crombie as that's how he always was.

Bill Crombie (Pictured) was to wave away a strong penalty claim in the game after Sandy Clark appeared to be tripped by Colin Hendry and, in his autobiography, Clark said:

"I believe the football authorities made an absolute mess of things by appointing Bill to our game.

"Everyone knew Bill was a Hearts fan. It put enormous pressure on him and it was all so unnecessary.

"I can't speak for Bill but it certainly looked like he was uncomfortable refereeing that Dens Park clash.

"The last thing he would have wanted was to be accused of favouritism towards Hearts. In that penalty call he went too far the other way

"I got a feeling it wasn't going to be our day. It all stemmed from the infamous penalty that never was after Colin Hendry brought me down. It came from a throw-in down our left.

"I turned Colin on the goal line and he stuck his thigh out and knocked me over. It was a stonewall penalty.

"If Bill had done his job right that day and given the correct decision then I believe Hearts would have won the league.

"I have met Bill on several occasions since but I have never been able to ask him why he never gave us that penalty. It still hurts so much.

"I don't really need to ask him because I know it should have been a penalty.

"It was such a momentous decision and one that I, Bill and every Hearts fan will have to live with for the rest of our lives."

Another person who was none too happy with Bill Crombie that day was his son Lawrence. So much so that it would be five years before they would speak again.

There was a general acceptance in Scottish football that season that Hearts would win the league since that had demolished Dundee Utd 3-0 at Tannadice in April 1986. Goals from Robertson (2) and Clark himself had seen Hearts end Dundee Utd's title challenge and do it in a way that suggested they would be unstoppable in their march to the Premier League championship. Celtic had an average, at best, season. Knocked out of both cups at Easter Road (By one of the worst Hibs teams ever) their form had been patchy at best. Indeed through one three week run, they were battered by Dundee Utd (3-0), Aberdeen (4-1) and Rangers (3-0) in the autumn with nothing suggesting that any sort of title challenge could be mounted. Hearts, on the other hand, had a terrible start to the season. Ironically Hearts and Celtic met each other on the opening day of season 85/86 and fought out a 1-1 draw at Tynecastle, with Paul McStay getting a last minute equaliser for Celtic. The following week Hearts visited Love Street and were battered 6-2 by St Mirren despite John Colquhoun opening the scoring, as he had done the previous week against Celtic, Hearts were 3-1 down at half time and 6-1 down in 72 minutes and not many eyebrows were raised given the yoyo status the team had made their own over the previous two decades. Things continued as normal for Hearts, they lost a few games, beat Hibs and generally peaked little interest from anyone outside Gorgie. Indeed those who attended a mundane draw 1-1 versus Dundee at Tynecastle on October 5th 1985 would have had little notion that this game would be the start of a 31 game unbeaten run that would take Hearts to the brink of what would be a league title for the first time since 1960. Hearts grew throughout the season. A 1-0 win at Celtic Park the following week was the first in three decades and sent shockwaves round Scottish football. Scotland's involvement in a two game play-off versus Australia in order to qualify for the 1986 World Cup in

Mexico meant that several games were cancelled in the top flight of Scottish football to accommodate the games and players travelling. Except none involving Hearts. A 2-0 win at Ibrox on the 28th of December 1985 all but ended Rangers challenge and meant that Hearts would be well clear at the top going in to 1986 and with wins at Celtic Park and Ibrox already under their belt, people were taking them seriously. A win at Pittodrie on January 18th 1986, a time when away team wins in Aberdeen were about as frequent as Haley's Comet, merely underlined their title credentials and by the time that emphatic win had come at Tannadice, hot on the heels of beating Dundee Utd 1-0 at Hampden in the Scottish Cup semi-final, very few people doubted that Hearts would win the league and probably the Scottish Cup as well. Indeed two books had already been penned (*The Boys in Maroon* by John Fairgrieve and *Glorious Hearts* by Mike Aitken) in anticipation of a Hearts triumph and the Hearts song had been released by the Hearts squad featuring Colin Chisholm and the Glasgow Branch of the Hearts supporters club which included a B side with the players singing "Championees, Championees oh we are, we are, we" and, ironically, the song was sponsored by "Marshalls: The Chunky Chicken Champions"

Interestingly, on the cover of the record, along with manager Alex MacDonald and player-assistant manager Sandy Jardine, was Wallace Mercer, owner of Hearts and long-time member of the Edinburgh Establishment. A resident of Essex Road in Barnton, Wallace would be pivotal in a certain David Murray getting to the top of the Edinburgh Establishment tree, but that's another book.

There was also the small matter of Edinburgh now being teeming with Hearts supporters. Many would say that a lot of Rangers supporters jumped from the sinking Ibrox ship and bolstered the numbers at Tynecastle whilst it's safe to say that sales of new Hearts scarves have never been higher. It felt like a procession and it is fair to assume that most in Scottish football, outside of Easter Road of course, weren't that unhappy about Hearts winning the league. Particularly when their closest challengers were Celtic. As has been said, Rangers were an utter shambles at the time. They would finish 5th in 1985/86 and celebrate the fact that a UEFA Cup place had been secured. Aberdeen's golden era was coming to an end but the heights achieved are noted by the fact that in season 1985/86 they won the League Cup and the Scottish Cup but it was seen as failure.

In the week leading up to the final league game in Scotland, it is often forgotten that Hearts could have won the league on April 30th 1986, the Wednesday before that fateful day at Dens Park. Celtic were visiting Fir Park for a game versus Motherwell where they knew anything other than a victory would see Hearts crowned Champions. Celtic had a mission beyond just winning that night, they wanted to put a big hole in Hearts superior goal difference, against a Motherwell side that had struggled all season, so to get within two points of Hearts and have a chance of winning the title on goal difference. No one at Hearts knew quite what chain of events would be triggered by Celtic's second goal that night. The second goal in a 2-0 win that most observers thought wouldn't be enough to help stop Hearts seemingly relentless charge to the title, their previous game a 1-0 win versus Clydebank being their 31st game in a row without defeat. The second goal that night for Celtic, scored by Brian McClair, was a penalty, it was a penalty awarded by Jim McCluskey (Stewarton although born in and bred in Airdrie)

This penalty infuriated one prominent referee in Scotland. The protection of sources prevents the naming of this referee but shortly after the game he approached Jim McCluskey and asked "What did you gie them that penalty fir?" To which McCluskey replied "Because it was a penalty". This drew little with the accuser who replied "Aye, but it was the sort of penalty you could have got away with no gieing and if they bastards win the league on Saturday, it will be your fucking fault"

It was that night that, post Celtic's win, Bill Crombie's phone would ring. On the other end of the line was Maureen Cooper, one of the two people who decided which referee would referee a certain game. All referees in Scotland knew as early as March 1986 where they would be on May 3rd 1986.

In the early 80's UEFA sent out an edict that all association referees would need to complete The Cooper Test. A fitness test that would ensure all referees would be at a certain level of fitness before officiating a game.

Here is a definition:

The Cooper 12 minute run test is a popular field test used for measuring aerobic fitness. Developed in 1968 by Dr Ken Cooper, this fitness test was initially used to estimate the VO2max of military personnel. Dr Cooper discovered that there was a high correlation between a person's VO2max value and the distance they can run or walk. This test is still very popular in the military as it is used for determining basic fitness. Over the years, it has also been used by trainers and coaches to verify track and cardiovascular fitness.

Procedure of the Test

The Cooper 12 minute run fitness test requires little equipment. Marking cones, a stopwatch and an oval running track is sufficient to conduct the test. You will need to set the cones at specific intervals from each other, depending on your preference. Ensure the intervals are measured as you will require the total distance to measure VO2max. When the track has been set up, you can start running around it. The objective of this test is to run or walk as much as you can in the 12 minute period.

How to Calculate Your Score

It is best to have a coach or trainer present so they can record the time for you. At the end of 12 minutes the test is stopped, and the covered distance is measured. You should record the distance travelled in those 12 minutes in miles or kilometers. With the obtained result, you can calculate your VO2max level using the following formulas.

VO2max = (35.97 x miles) - 11.29 (in miles)

VO2max = (22.351 x kilometers) - 11.288 (in kilometers)

You can also compare your test results with the recommendations and norms of others in the same age and gender category as you. Remember that fitness levels for men and women are different.

The Cooper 12 minute run fitness test is an extremely advantageous fitness test. This is because it can be modified to suit all populations. As the result from this test is based on the length of time, you can run as well as walk during the allotted time. One of the biggest advantages of this test is that it can be performed by several people simultaneously. In addition to this, it is fairly inexpensive as it requires little equipment. Studies have shown that the Cooper 12 minute run fitness test is quite reliable. But the level of reliability also depends on pacing strategies, motivation level and practice. The reliability of this test also depends on how strictly the test is conducted.

The Cooper 12 minute run fitness test can be quite strenuous. For this reason, it is important that you get clearance by your physician before performing it. A short warm up of approximately 10-15 minutes before beginning is a must. Keep the warm up light as you are sure to get tired during the test. Stretching your muscles well before starting will be vital to the test. Once you are warmed up properly, the Cooper 12 minute run fitness test should commence.

The Cooper Test was adapted for Referees and involved three elements

1. a series of 10 metre shuttle runs

2. A 200 metre sprint

3. A 12 minute continuous run during which the referee had to cover a minimum distance of 2300 metres

The Maureen Cooper Test was slightly different. Maureen started at the SFA when they were based in West Regent Street in Glasgow. As secretary she dealt with all top flight referees, just in different ways. She was the person that a referee would post his expenses claim into, sometimes they would hand it in in person. Many referees would simply drop in for a "blether". Maureen was a good looking woman, tall, blonde hair, who carried herself well with a confidence that would often to lead to manipulation of others.

What Maureen Cooper wanted, Maureen Cooper got. Or who as the case may be.
She carried on lots of affairs with many referees in Scotland, a lot of whom were married men, but this did not bother her, she was married herself. Her success rate with referees was such that a buzz phrase hung around her like fly paper on a hot day:

"Who is the current jockey?"

However misogynist that sounds, no one was in any doubt who called the shots in any relationship. It was Maureen Cooper always. When conducting an affair with a referee she would always go and watch said referee wherever he happened to be officiating in the country. What's more, her husband Tom would always accompany her to the games and however bizarre that sounds, it can only be so much compared to the fact that after the games Maureen Cooper would socialise with her husband and the current referee she was having an affair with. There was never any attempt to hide an affair and indeed anyone not knowing who the "current jockey" was would simply look at the fixtures, see who had been allocated the best ones and would mark up in their head another successful entrant in the Maureen Cooper Test. This is how games in

Scotland were allocated. Indeed when Maureen retired in 2009, she was given a glowing tribute for her years of service:

Best wishes to long serving Maureen

Friday 31st July 2009

It is an end of an era for referees as tomorrow's The Co-operative Insurance First Round matches were the last appointments to be made by Maureen Cooper, who has looked after the men in black for nearly half a century.

Cooper has retired after a 46 year career scheduling match officials and at a Dinner in her honour referees from throughout her time in office came to pay their thanks.

Maureen worked for the Scottish Football League for over 40 years before transferring to the SFA when the control refereeing appointments became their remit.

Peter Donald, the former Secretary of the SFL said, "When Maureen started working for us Third Lanark were still in the top Division so that gives you a measure of the change she has seen during her time. Maureen is respected by everyone that knows her and I wish her well in her retirement."

SFA Chief Executive Gordon Smith said, "Maureen showed extraordinary dedication to the Scottish game, in a remarkable 46-year-career. Her hard work over the years at both the Scottish Football League, and latterly, the Scottish FA, has been invaluable, and countless referees have benefited from Maureen's support and guidance. On behalf of everyone at the Scottish FA, I wish her all the best for a long and happy retirement."

If your face, or perhaps another part of your anatomy, fitted with Maureen Cooper, you got to referee who you wanted as it was Maureen Cooper who allocated games in Scotland, period.

Except Dundee v Hearts on Saturday May 3rd 1986.

Because although it was Maureen Cooper who made the call to Bill Crombie, it was in fact the other person who could have a say in allocated games to referees who made the decision to give the game to Bill Crombie a few days before it was due to be played. This person had no relationships with any referees, never socialised with referees and knew very little about football in general. He did know though that Bill Crombie was an avid Hearts supporter though, everyone at the SFA did and so it is up to us to judge after the question:

So why did Jim Farry decide substitute one referee, three days before the game, in order to put a well-known Hearts supporter in charge of a game that could see Hearts win the league for the first time since 1960?

Do you think, as Sandy Clark said, it was to *hinder* Hearts?

With that logic, maybe this renowned football man used his immense football knowledge and wanted to *help* Celtic by ensuring Jorge Cadete didn't play against Rangers in April 1996?

Jim Farry had probably never even heard of Albert Kidd before May 3rd 1986.

It is safe to assume that he did after it.

Freemasonry And The Lanarkshire Referees Association

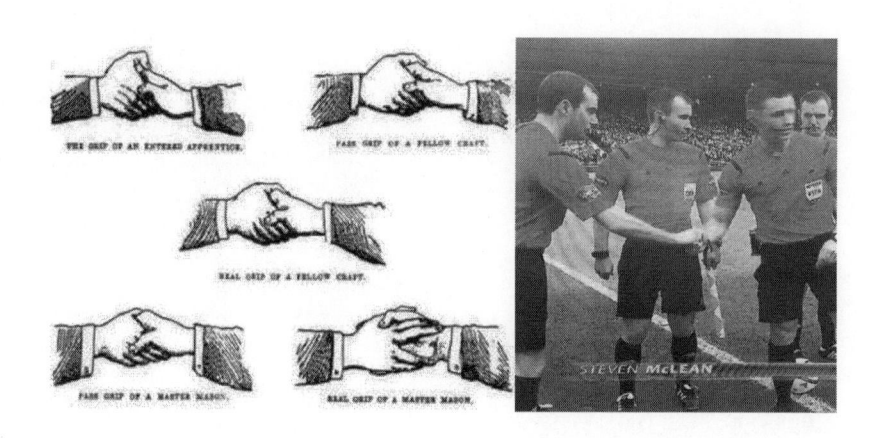

The publication of the Macpherson report in February 1999 is regarded by many as a defining moment in British race relations. The report by Sir William Macpherson followed an inquiry into the Metropolitan police's investigation of the murder of a black teenager, Stephen Lawrence. The 18-year-old A-Level student was fatally stabbed in an unprovoked attack as he waited for a bus in Eltham, south London, in April 1993. Allegations of incompetence and racism against Metropolitan police officers in charge of the case soured race relations as did two internal police inquiries which exonerated the Met itself. The Macpherson report delivered a damning assessment of the "institutional racism" within the Metropolitan police and policing generally. It made 70 recommendations many aimed specifically at improving police attitudes to racism and stressed the importance of a rapid increase in the numbers of black and Asian police officers. The government pledged to increase the number of officers from minority ethnic groups from around 2,500 to 8,000 by 2009.

But a survey carried out on the second anniversary of the Macpherson report in February revealed only 155 new officers from ethnic minority had been recruited in the past year compared to an increase of 261 in the year following the report. Thirteen forces had either failed to recruit a single Asian or black officer or had seen their numbers fall. In spite of the lack of progress in recruiting ethnic minority officers a year after the publication of the Macpherson report public perceptions of the police appeared to be changing. A survey of more than 1,200 people showed that three quarters believed the police had learnt from the Stephen Lawrence case and only 3% believed the police were 'very racist'. In response to heavy criticism in Sir William's report, an independent police authority was set up in July 2000 to oversee the Metropolitan police which had been the only force in England and Wales not to be monitored by such a body. The Met also set up an independent advisory group to advise it on race issues. But, in February of 2001, four black members of the group resigned, saying they had been reduced to being "nodding dogs". In their resignation letter the four said that the group was controlled by the police and had lost its independence and credibility as well as recommendations relating to the police, the Macpherson report also proposed changing some laws.

In January 2012 a Home Office report said that a black person in London was five times more likely than a white person to be stopped by the police.

There has never been an inquiry into the role of the Grand Lodge of Scotland in refereeing.

A chant that has emanated round the terraces and stands of Celtic games since the 60's has been "Who's the Mason in the black" (I guess it started to die down a bit in the modern era, not because there was any less belief that the referees were masons, more that the colour of their attire changed)

It is one thing to say it another to prove it. First of all, let's look at how the Grand Lodge of Scotland defines itself:

Freemasonry is one of the world's oldest secular fraternal societies and which originated in Scotland. Below we explain Freemasonry as it exists under the Grand Lodge of Scotland which is the corporate body governing Freemasonry in Scotland and Scottish Masonic Lodges in many other parts of the world.

Freemasonry is a society of men concerned with moral and spiritual values. Its members are taught its precepts by a series of ritual dramas. These remain substantially the same form used in Scottish stonemasons lodges, and use Scottish stonemasons' customs and tools as allegorical guides.

The essential qualification for admission into and continuing membership is a belief in a Supreme Being. Membership is open to men of any race or religion who can fulfil this essential qualification and who are of good repute.

Freemasonry is not a religion, nor is it a substitute for religion. The one essential qualification means that Freemasonry is open to men of many religions and it expects and encourages them to continue to follow their own faith. It is not permitted for Freemasons to discuss religion at Masonic meetings.

For many years Freemasons have followed three great principles:

Brotherly Love

Every true Freemason will show tolerance and respect for the opinions of others and behave with kindness and understanding to his fellow creatures.

Relief

Freemasons are taught to practise charity and to care - not only for their own - but also for the community as a whole, both by charitable giving and by voluntary efforts and works as individuals.

Truth

Freemasons strive for truth, requiring high moral standards and aiming to achieve them in their own lives. Freemasons believe that these principles represent a way of achieving higher standards in life.

A Freemason is encouraged to do his duty first to his God (by whatever name he is known) through his faith and religious practice; and then, without detriment to his family and those dependent on him, to his neighbour through charity and service. *None of these ideas is exclusively Masonic, but all should be universally acceptable. Freemasons are expected to follow them.*

That's the official line but the key sentence is highlighted.

A sense of duty is instilled into a Mason from day one. Clearly that scope can go far and wide, especially in refereeing in Lanarkshire.

*

A young man who wanted to become a referee was given contact details for his local Referees Association, arranged to go to the next class and joined about 20 hopefuls for the three month course. Everything was positive and the trainees were told that the only barriers to succeeding in refereeing were the limit of your ability and your commitment.

How that statement would be ripped apart in the years to come.

After passing the exam – which had a daunting 80% pass mark – he was invited to the monthly Association Meeting to receive his Certificate and Badge.

He prepared himself for a strong firm handshake but was a wee bit put out by the President's thumb pressing on his knuckle and an awkward repositioning of hands took place – this was a 'handshake' he would meet many times and would become expert in returning 'the grip'

Going to Meetings

It took him longer to realise the significance of some comments from senior referees.

"You going on Thursday?"

"Where were you on Monday night?"

It took a while for him to realise that these other nights were not additional training sessions but Masonic meetings in various places across the County.

What's in a name?

During his first season in the Juniors he was appointed to a match involving a team considered to have leanings towards the East End of Glasgow. After the match one of the Committee spoke to him.

"Are you new in the Juniors? I thought you had a good game, I'll let the Match Secretary know."

Another Committee man butted in

"For fuck sake don't dae that. If we praise a referee wi' a name like his we will never see him again."

"Okay" says the first committee man "I'll phone and say ye were shite"

The next time he spoke to the Match Secretary he was made aware of being criticised but was told "Don't you worry , I let they bastards know that it is me that appoints referees and they will not dictate to me who not to appoint"

OOPS.

As he made his way through the Junior leagues he was struck by just how often he was greeted by 'the handshake'. Their insistence on giving 'the grip' led to an amusing experience.

Although he had a game of his own that day he was asked to do an early morning mid- winter pitch inspection before an important league game. The match referee was unavailable and as a big crowd was expected he was asked to check out the pitch at 9am.

He arrived to be met by two Committee Men.

"How come you're here? You're no the match referee!"

"He's not available but he will be here this afternoon if the game is on"

"Thank fuck it's you. We are at full strength the day and we hear they huv three men missing. We reckon we can do them if the game's on and that Fenian bastard would put it aff just tae spite us"

He said nothing, asked for a ball, walked onto the park and booted the ball in the air. It landed with a 'splatt' He kicked it again and it stuck in water. Lifting the ball, he simply said:

"Game's off. I'll phone the Match Secretary"

"Fur fuck's sake we thought you wid dae us a turn" At that they started to walk away.

"Excuse me, gentleman. You forgot to pay me the Inspection Fee"

Grudgingly a cheque was written but he handed it back to them.

"Sorry but that's not my name. My name is xxxxxxxxx."

A look of shock came over them as they realised they had mistaken him for one of the handshake brigade from Lanarkshire who had recently attended a meeting at their local Lodge.

The Three Degrees – Lanarkshire Style

It was common practice in Lanarkshire to encourage up and coming referees to join the masons. Guys who had shown no interest suddenly developed a new handshake and were busy on certain evenings as they had "a meeting to go to"

We have heard on the grapevine of one unsuccessful attempt at recruitment.

A group of Referees from Lanarkshire Referees Association took a young ref for a drink to celebrate promotion to the Senior List of Referees as a Linesman. A lot of backslapping and a few pints later the conversation got a wee bit serious.

"Right, that's you on the List so we will arrange to get you in to the freemasons."

"Why would I want in?"

"Because it will help you to be seen at the right meetings by the people that matter."

"What do you mean you will arrange to get me in?"

"We will organise it and make sure you don't get blackballed"

"Why would I get blackballed?"

"Because you are a Catholic, but we will get it fixed"

"If that is what I need to do to get on in refereeing, you can stick it up your arse"

Influence of 'The Craft"

Meeting referees and linesmen from other Associations, particularly when meeting Lanarkshire referees for the first time, brought home to our source how widespread membership of 'The Craft' was and he lost count of the number of times he was asked 'How old is yer Granny?' after he had made an attempt at returning the infamous handshake. Although on the surface this seemed like a very polite and friendly question it was another of the 'brother masons' codes to find out what Lodge you belonged to.

The number of referees on the SFA's Senior List of Referees with Masonic links is way out of line with the number of Freemasons in Scotland.

It is estimated that in 2013 there were about 22,000 Freemasons in Scotland. This represents approximately 1 in every 100 adult males. Don't ask me the source of this information, because it is a secret, but 100% reliable.

On this basis you would expect only a couple of the Referees and Assistant Referees on the SFA List to be masons. The reality, as we know is something entirely different.

Brother Tait

The first time the source of this book met and shared a dressing room with Bobby Tait his first impressions were of a really sociable and likeable guy who was down to earth and not "up his own arse" like many of the Grade 1 referees. However, the 'handshake' was predictable. The pre-match chat was very friendly and then they headed to the dressing room.
As they were getting their referees kit on our man noticed that, like many refs and indeed players, Tait put on two pairs of socks before putting his football boots on. No problem there you might think. However, while the outer pair were the standard referee socks, black with white tops, it was the other socks that drew his attention.

Black socks with red tops – now where had our ref seen these before?

"Is it not dodgy wearing Rangers socks under your Referee socks?"

"I've worn these in every game since I was a boy and I'm not going to stop now. Anyway, who is going to report me?"

End of conversation.

The system is delivered with a 'helping hand'.

The creeping influence of the Carluke Masonic connection of Cumming, McVicar and Morrison with their other Lanarkshire Brothers Crossley and Dallas show that a small but powerful group can exert undue control and influence on organisations and society.

Look no further than the masonic influence on Scottish football in general and refereeing in particular.

(Derek Parlane and Derek Johnstone-The sentence underneath this photo find read "We had a visit in January from two famous Rangers Brethren, they had asked to visit the lodge and were struck by its magnificence"

Of course, there is good old Bobby Tait (East Kilbride). Andy Goram tells a story that, when he first arrived at Ibrox, he was staggered by the familiarity between referees and the staff at Ibrox. Indeed one referee approached him and said the words "Welcome to the big club, good luck, you won't need it though" before giving him a funny handshake.

That referee was Bobby Tait (East Kilbride).

The bizarre notion that referees are fans of football rather than football fans is laughable in any area where there is a

133

concentration of big football clubs with Lanarkshire as typical an area as any in Scotland. With four senior football clubs it does give officials the chance to nominate a pet club but over 90% of those interested in football from the area support Celtic or Rangers.

Starting their careers at a similar time were two budding young whistlers, Bobby Tait from East Kilbride and Kevin O'Donnell from Coatbridge. With their interest in the game taking them into refereeing they discovered some handy pocket money, a way to keep fit and get closer to the game they grew up playing- and supporting their favourite teams.

As they moved through the ranks, the hard school of junior football navigated they began to get a foothold in the senior game, being linesmen at lower division matches or refereeing reserve team matches.

Bobby Tait's support for Rangers was well known, joked about and out in the open, O'Donnell found that his name immediately led to suspicions that he may not be one of the boys with any preference for Celtic having to be well disguised and kept under wraps.

*

With Brian Robertson, another East Kilbride based referee retiring and moving into a supervisor role Bobby Tait's career through the ranks was assured. O'Donnell had no such mentor.

After a few top division matches O'Donnell was given the Celtic v Hearts fixture on the second day on the 1987/88 season. A late goal from Mark McGhee, who specialised in scoring in this fixture, won the match for Celtic with Hearts owner Wallace Mercer leaving no-one in any doubt about the reason for his side's defeat.

At the time, pre David Murray, Mercer was the biggest noise in the game with the media happy to relay every sound bite. It wasn't a red card or a penalty that upset the Hearts chairman, it was a run of the mill challenge with McGhee well known for using his ample backside to his advantage.

By the time October came around O'Donnell had dropped off the circuit for Premier League matches, faced with a wall of silence and no explanation for his career coming to a halt he packed in refereeing appearing for a short time as a lower division reporter for Radio Clyde.

On the other side of the fence was Bobby Tait (East Kilbride), good old Bobby, everyone knew what side he cheered for but that was all a bit of a laugh, never affected him on the pitch, applied the laws of the game fairly and squarely, it was time keeping that was his problem.

In February 98, with a three horse race to the title he conjured up four minutes of extra time for Jose Quitingo to come up with a stoppage time equaliser for Hearts. As Celtic restarted, with Morten Wieghorst bearing into the Hearts box Bobby Tait (East Kilbride) found his whistle for full time.

Two months later as Jim Jefferies side indulged in an exhibition of time wasting Stephane Mahe was treated for three minutes before being stretchered off. Bobby Tait (East Kilbride) added 30 seconds stoppage time with the match finishing goal-less.

Karma, however, is one son of a bitch and Bobby Tait (East Kilbride) felt it bite his backside big time on the second last weekend of the season. Being part of the furniture, Bobby Tait (East Kilbride) got his wish to finish up at his favourite ground the East Kilbride based referee got Rangers v Kilmarnock, also a farewell day for nine-in-a-row legends like Brian Laudrup, Richard Gough, Ally McCoist, Stuart McCall and of course Walter Smith.

Wins in their final two matches would have turned nine into ten, as Bobby Tait (East Kilbride) fully appreciated. As the final whistle blew across the country they continued playing and playing at Ibrox, nil-nil was the score. Finally four minutes into stoppage time there was a goal- Ally Mitchell scored for the visitors, Ibrox emptied, the legends came out to take a bow in front of a few hundred fans with Bobby Tait (East Kilbride) refereeing his last ever match the following week at Cliftonhill, in the home town of O'Donnell, forced out of football a decade earlier.

Bobby Tait (East Kilbride) now revels in tales of his Rangers minded refereeing on the after dinner circuit, Rangers 'charity' events being a specialty.

Only in Scotland.

The Dallas Cowboys

The main character in the Netflix drama, adapted from the UK series, *House of Cards*, is Frank Underwood. The viewer learns very quickly that Frank is unscrupulous, ruthless and unrelenting in his pursuit of power and will manipulate anyone and everyone to achieve his ultimate goal, to be President of the United States of America. Hugh Dallas (Bonkle) had slightly less ambition, he would just wanted to be the top man in refereeing in Scotland but his methods to get there were very similar to that of the fictional Frank Underwood. Hugh Dallas (Bonkle) was your best friend until the second you couldn't do anything for him and then he would drop you like a bad singer on X Factor.

Dallas latched onto whichever individual or group within refereeing who could help to get him promoted to the next level. When someone had reached the limit of their influence and could no longer help his next upwards move, Dallas looked for a new friend, or 'brother', who would provide favourable reports or introductions at the next level.

It has been said that it was his diligence and willing within Masonic circles that helped Hugh Dallas up the refereeing ladder. He started refereeing in 1982 in the amateur game. His first game was Motherwell Bridgeworks v Victoria AFC. He enraged all who saw his performance that day, sending off three and booking six and received a torrent of abuse from some spectators. His fee was £6. With the Jack Mowat (Burnside) regime having given way to Frank Crossley (Wishaw) regime, Hugh had to get up the ladder that we now know wasn't going to be through refereeing excellence.

Despite many people in Lanarkshire having serious doubts about his ability a series of Supervisory Reports were carried out by his 'friends' who had influence and Dallas was surprisingly for some promoted to referee in Juniors football in what was then the Central League which has now been merged into the West Region of the SJFA.

Jock Gray (Cambuslang) was the match secretary for the Central League. He was not in the spring of youth when Hugh Dallas (Bonkle) was an up and coming referee. Thing is, Hugh Dallas wasn't looking for the benefit of the Jock Gray's refereeing experience. He wanted the benefit of his connections. And what were those connections? Well Jock Gray was a high ranking Mason and Hugh Dallas knew this. So driving Jock to the supermarket and cash and carry were no problem, "anything for Jock Gray", and he was lifted and laid by Hugh Dallas when it came to going to his frequent Masonic meetings as well. So Hugh Dallas was being looked upon kindly by masonic eyes and in one of those freak occurrences, at the same time, his refereeing career started to blossom.

Key appointments to high profile junior matches were guaranteed for "Auld Jock's Chauffeur" and with his mentors Cumming, McVicar and Co sending carefully selected Supervisors to ensure the reports were tailor made to push him up the rankings we had the perfect storm brewing to drive Dallas to the top of the refereeing pile.

Dallas would climb the ranks in Scotland and within the walls of UEFA as well.

This was despite being involved in, and directly responsible for, one of the most controversial games on Scottish football history.

May 2nd 1999, Celtic versus Rangers, Celtic Park,

The scenario was simple, if Rangers won the game, they would win the league.

Celtic started well enough but it was obvious a pattern was emerging and many onlookers were absolutely convinced that Hugh Dallas had a vendetta against Celtic left back, Stephane Mahe.

Rangers took the lead on 12 minutes, through the Neil McCann, but Celtic continued to make chances despite a badly depleted team. Mahe was rampaging down the left at will and looked in the mood. Yet by 31 minutes he was red carded Hugh Dallas after two yellow cards, one after reacting to an outrageous tackle by Neil McCann. The venom Hugh Dallas showed towards the Celtic player enraged the Celtic support. There had always been suspicions about how Dallas felt about Celtic but nothing would compare to the fury that would erupt on 40 minutes. Awarding Rangers a corner, Dallas inexplicably walked over to Rangers player Giovanni Van Bronckhurst and patted him on the behind. This was at the corner I was sitting at, although quite high up, and I can remember the looks of astonishment that surrounded me. It was too much for one fan who ran on the park to try to get Hugh Dallas. Whilst that can't be condoned, I can't honestly sit here and say I wouldn't have done the same had I been in a position to. One fan even remonstrated so passionately that he fell from an upper tier of the stand.

Then, as things threatened to get completely out of hand, Dallas was struck on the head with a coin.

As things eventually calmed down, the corner was taken and Hugh Dallas awarded Rangers a penalty. I've watched the incident back about 10 times and have yet to see any infringement. Indeed Paul Lambert immediately said to Dallas "You've gave that because of the coin" whilst pointing at his head.

Rangers scored the penalty and went on to win 3-0, win the league and mock The Huddle in the process.

Something that was instigated by Neil McCann.

The game was played at 6.05pm on the Sunday of a bank holiday weekend and the Police blamed alcohol and vowed the game would never kick off again at that time. A problem they would only have until 2012.

The Celtic Wiki writes:

Reduced by a ridiculous amount of injuries, the writing was on the wall from kick off in a game that had to be won. Dallas had a record of being less than partial towards Celtic. The match had been hyped by SKY for nearly two weeks. With the match kicking off at 18:05 on a Sunday (for the benefit of SKY) everyone had been at the bar all afternoon. The ensuing response from the crowd was ugly but somewhat predictable given these conditions, the championship deciding nature of the game, the warm weather, the booze and the 'antagonism' towards Rangers. The debate about the game went on for a long time, with the media going into absolute feeding frenzy, their self-righteousness knowing no bounds. The events led to a change in all subsequent arrangements for Glasgow derbies.

The SFA launched an immediate inquiry into the game and events. Dallas had his windows smashed that night. A night of mayhem followed with clashes all over the place and hospital Casualty Departments full. And politicians called for immediate action.

Celtic CEO Allan MacDonald sent a video of the game to Chris Lewis of London-based consultants Anderson Lewis Associated. His report was sent to the SFA and SPL, who decide what Refs control these games.

The shrink's trial-by-telly verdict was that Dallas sparked the riot by using "over- friendly" gestures to Rangers players and MacDonald claimed: "The study of his body language came to the conclusion he was capable of provoking the kind of crowd reaction we don't want to see inside Celtic Park. "Was it purely co-incidental that shortly after he was seen patting Gio van Bronckhorst a coin came on to the park and struck the referee? "Not according to the careful scrutiny of the game carried out by a man trained to understand crowd reactions and the reasons for them."

Celtic's chief executive denied they want to ruin the ref's career or have him blacklisted for the March 2000 derby and said: "All we wanted to do by involving a psychologist was help make a good referee an even better one."

Celtic had already asked the SPL to axe Dallas as ref for the 1999 December 21 clash.

An SPL spokesman said at the time "I can confirm our Football Board did receive a psychologist's report on Hugh Dallas as part of Celtic's request to have a change of referee for the game in December. Since the meeting to discuss that matter was held in confidence we must take the view that our response to this story has to be kept confidential too." He said Celtic were searching for a world class referee to scrutinise the full May 2 match and report back to Celtic chief Allan MacDonald with his findings.

We all know what Hugh Dallas did that day at Celtic Park. Do we know what he did the day after that day at Celtic Park?

Well, there were these two guys, Calum Murray and Bill McDonald who ran Beazer Homes Partnership based in Cumbernauld, affordable homes, a very profitable business. Calum was the Managing Director.

Watson & Dallas (Hugh) provided most of their exterior doors right through, well, let's call them 'The Asterisk Years'

Bill McDonald got the Job of Technical Director 'Designate' of Beazer Homes mainstream housing and is the sort of guy who would never hide his anti-Celtic and anti-Irish/Catholic hatred.

For example, he would stand behind people he knew were Catholics and/or Celtic supporters whistling *The Sash* hoping for a reaction. With Bill it was a constant Tim this, Taig that and so on.

Described by someone who has worked with him for years as a "horrid human being"

In work that Monday, as employees made small talk about the game and how bad their hangovers were, one employee glanced out the window and there in front of him is the bold Hugh Dallas striding in and heading to reception.

He exchanges "hellos" in the foyer and excuses himself to go to the bathroom.

There is a huge open space room which faces Bill McDonald's 'glass' room in the corner.

When Bill sees Hugh he is ecstatic and greets him heartily whereas Hugh is a little bashful.

Why was Hugh Dallas there? He could only be with Bill for one thing, orders of external doors, he was getting orders from Beazer Partnership and now Bill was going to give him the mainstream (normal) Beazer Homes Scotland West contracts, why else would he be there on this day of all days?

Is it possible a Ref could use influence on the field for influence off it?

Oh and Calum Murray? Well he now works at UK CCG (http://c-c-g.co.uk/)

Only other employee I know of that company is below:

145

Incidentally, that day Hugh noticed that everyone in that office called Bill by another name, "Monkfish" Being an inquisitive sort of chap, Hugh asked "why do you call him Monkfish?"

"Because he looks like one"

Hugh Dallas would go on to be embroiled in the "Dougie, Dougie" affair where he concoct a conspiracy to mislead the Celtic manager at the time, Neil Lennon.

He survived that but then was caught sending an deeply offensive email from his official SFA email account which mocked The Pope and made light of child abuse.

Of course, when Hugh Dallas was caught sending a deeply offensive email mocking Pope Benedict Scotland's reaction was typical: Nothing to see here, move on. Indeed it took the Catholic Church in Scotland to speak out before anything was actually done.

Head of referee development Hugh Dallas has been sacked by the Scottish Football Association after being accused of sending a tasteless e-mail.
The former World Cup referee was the subject of an internal disciplinary hearing on Thursday evening.
SFA chief executive Stewart Regan investigated reports of an email sent from Dallas's SFA account when the Pope visited Scotland on 16 September.
And, on Wednesday, a Catholic Church spokesman called on the SFA to act.
BBC Radio 5 live reported that three other SFA staff members have been dismissed, with formal warnings issued to three more.

The Catholic Church urged Scottish football's governing body to sack Dallas if it was proved he had passed on a "tasteless message" relating to the Pope's visit to Scotland.

Following Regan's investigation, the former referee was said to be taking a few days out to consider his future and the SFA added that it would not comment until that process was completed.
BBC Scotland had seen the email in question.

It was sent from the SFA account belonging to 53-year-old Dallas, contained no text but included an image attachment of a school crossing sign with a silhouette of an adult holding a child's hand and the word "caution".

Beneath the road sign were words making reference to the Pope's arrival in Scotland.

While Regan was said to have returned to his Yorkshire home, SFA president George Peat said he could not comment on Dallas's departure.
"
Stewart Regan has interviewed a number of people at Hampden," he told BBC Scotland.

"I have not been in there (on Friday). I stayed away from there because, if he has dismissed anyone, any appeal from people who have been dismissed would come to me.

"I don't know if people have gone or not - that is possible.

"Some people have phoned me and told me that five have left, but I don't know how many have gone and who they might be. I don't want to get involved."

Dallas, who had been the SFA's head of referee development since June 2009, had also been under pressure in recent weeks following criticism from factions within Scottish football directed at match officials.

Celtic, in particular, had been angered by referee Dougie McDonald's decision to overturn his own award of a penalty against Dundee United on 17 October. The SFA launched an investigation after assistant Steven Craven resigned as a result of the furore and McDonald was warned for giving a false explanation for his decision.

Craven accused Dallas of "bullying and harrassment" over the incident, although that was strenuously denied by both the referees' chief and McDonald.

Although Regan promised an overhaul of referee discipline, Celtic continued to call for tougher action taken against McDonald, with chairman John Reid calling on the referee to resign or be sacked. Reid alluded to what he claimed was a history of bias against Celtic and supported MP Pete Wishart's suggestion that referees should reveal which football teams they support.

Celtic had also recently written to the SFA asking for clarification over a penalty awarded against them by Willie Collum during the Old Firm derby against Rangers.

Following that incident, striker Gary Hooper suggested that referees wanted to give decisions against his club.

Then, this week, Scotland's referees withdrew their labour ahead of this weekend's fixtures, complaining of undue pressure, abuse and that their integrity was being questioned.

Both Dallas and the SFA were unavailable for comment tonight. The SFA have made no official comment all day despite both Polish and Portuguese officials withdrawing their offers to cover for striking refs.

of the striking category one referees, John McKendrick, described the departure of Dallas as a "very dark day for referees in Scotland". "We have to remember that Hugh Dallas was a world-class operator," he said.

Pictures of Dallas, crouched on one knee with blood streaming from a head wound, are one of the most stark images in Scottish football.

In 1999, during a title decider in which three players were sent off and a penalty was awarded to Rangers, Dallas was struck on the head by a coin thrown from the Celtic section of support.

Celtic subsequently hired a behavioural psychologist to investigate Dallas's behaviour in the match.

Dallas was awarded an MBE for services to football a few months after being chosen to be the fourth official at the 2002 World Cup final.

Even though Dallas was sacked for sending the email there was still a feeling that the SFA really weren't taking this seriously and only bowed to public pressure rather than have any real indignation themselves. Indeed, in this press piece, George Peat doesn't really seem to get it at all.

THE offensive e-mail that led to referee chief Hugh Dallas leaving the Scottish Football Association is just the "tip of the iceberg" of anti-Catholic feeling in Scotland, Church leaders have claimed.

Peter Kearney, director of the Scottish Catholic Media Office, said the e-mail was an example of "deep, wide and vicious anti-Catholic hostility".

Meanwhile, the wider crisis engulfing Scottish referees took a dramatic twist last night with the resignation of Dougie McDonald, the man whose admission that he misled Celtic boss Neil Lennon over his decision to rescind a penalty triggered the current controversy.

Having called last week for Mr Dallas to be sacked if it was proved he forwarded the e-mail that suggested the Pope was a risk to children, Mr Kearney has now said "the bigotry, bile, sectarian undercurrents and innuendos must end".

He said similar e-mails circulated in the weeks leading up to Pope Benedict's visit to Scotland highlighted the level of anti-Catholic feeling in Scotland.

Writing in a Sunday newspaper, he said: "Of the 2,000 or so Catholic priests who have worked in Scotland over the past 25 years, fewer than one in 200 has been convicted of sexual abuse. I am disturbed that in a country where more than 99 per cent of Catholic clergy are innocent of any offence, they can be subjected to so much hate-fueled scorn. I would challenge critics to provide evidence of any other profession with such an exemplary record."

He claimed anti-Catholic bigotry had existed in Scotland for hundreds of years and urged Scottish Catholics to speak out against it. "It has existed since the Reformation and its viciousness was renewed and deepened when the first Irish migrants arrived a century and a half ago," Mr Kearney wrote.

"Our grandparents and even our parents suffered intolerance and persecution. We will not tolerate it. We will not laugh it off - because there is no funny side."

Reports suggest Mr Dallas, who left his post as head of referee development on Friday, and four other staff members who have also been disciplined are considering suing the SFA for unfair dismissal. The other staff are reported to be Craig Levein's secretary Amanda Macdonald, mailroom boss Bob Bryan, Marco McIntyre from football development and Tim Berridge, an audio visual technician.

The SFA said it had not yet received any appeals.

Its president, George Peat, told The Scotsman affected staff members had five days to appeal the decision. "I saw the four names in the paper today, but I honestly don't know whether they are involved or not," he said."I've tried to stay out of it. If anyone has a grievance or wants to appeal, it'll come to me. I deliberately *didn't ask about the identities of the staff so I couldn't be accused of getting involved at this stage."*

SFA chief executive Stewart Regan also refused to confirm the names of the staff members who had left.

In response to Mr Kearney's comments, he said: "This was not about anti-Catholicism, in my view. It's about appropriate use of our e-mail and internet, and a decision was taken in relation to abuse of that policy."

Mr Regan has been in post for only six weeks, having recently moved from Yorkshire County Cricket, and said he could not comment on allegations that sectarianism was rife in Scotland or in Scottish football.

He said tackling sectarianism was not the responsibility of the SFA. "We're a football organisation and our job is to deal with football issues," he said.

Mr Regan launched his investigation after reports of the e-mail emerged earlier this month.

The e-mail apparently included a photograph showing a road sign featuring an adult and child with a doctored message below referring to the Pope's visit.

Last Wednesday, Mr Kearney wrote to Mr Regan, suggesting Mr Dallas should be sacked if it was proved he had sent the "gratuitously insulting" e-mail.

George Peat is well known to Celtic fans. As well numerous public utterances that at times made him look like David Murray's PR man. We all know about his campaign to extend the league season in 2008 to, let's face it, help Rangers win the league. One other, slightly less known, story gives a further insight into the character of George Peat. At a meeting to discuss the Airdrie ticket allocation for a Scottish Cup tie at Celtic Park in January 1999. Peat had one agenda: To ensure the ticket price would be £25. Celtic were exasperated by his stance and eventually someone to him "Look George, £25 is an outrageous price for a Scottish Cup tie against a team from a lower league" to which Peat replied "I don't care, it's Celtic supporters who will be paying it"

Even as he was ready to leave office, he still had to pin his colours to the mast one last time:

Celtic seem certain to call for the resignation of George Peat, president of the Scottish Football Association, after it emerged he was in attendance when the decision to impose a six-match touchline ban on Neil Lennon was taken.

The original suspension, meted out on January 11 by the SFA's disciplinary committee after an outburst aimed at Steven McLean, the fourth official, during the Clydesdale Bank Premier League game against Hearts in November, was reduced to four games at an appeals board hearing chaired by Lord Carloway on at Hampden on Thursday.

Celtic are still awaiting Lord Carloway's full written findings, but Herald Sport can outline the full facts behind what actually went on throughout the case.

Peat, who is to step down in the summer and be replaced by Campbell Ogilvie, is certain to come under heavy fire again from the Celtic hierarchy for his part in proceedings.

Herald Sport can reveal that, despite assurances he was only there as an observer when Lennon was originally tried, Peat actually went into the room along with the four members of the disciplinary committee when they retired to deliberate on what the punishment should be.

The SFA's legal team, fronted by Ronnie Clancy QC, insisted under cross examination from Lord Carloway that Peat had no involvement in the decision-making process but, crucially, they could not explain why he was in the room in the first place.

At a four-and-a-half hour hearing the QC acting on Lennon's behalf, Paul McBride, dismantled the SFA's case -- and asked why Peat was even involved as it was a matter for the disciplinary committee.

McBride also probed the reasons why the SFA would not provide him with all the fine detail, statements and evidence of previous 'excessive misconduct' cases brought against managers on a first charge -- something he felt was crucial as it would clearly outline precedence.

He was left to find these himself in the media, but was denied the detail of what had been said by the individuals to match officials in order for punishments to be set.

These flaws, and Peat's involvement on the day, led to Lord Carloway setting aside, in its entirety, the full hearing of January 11. Effectively, while Lennon always had a case to answer, key procedural matters had not been followed and, therefore, the case against him was absolutely flawed.

Lord Carloway suggested a new punishment be brought; a mandatory two-game ban for being sent to the stand, and an additional two for swearing at McLean. This was accepted by all parties.

However, a senior Parkhead source said last night: "The bottom line is George Peat should have been nowhere near that hearing but he chose to be there. As SFA president, it was argued he had a right to be there as an observer. But why was he in the room when the decision to hand out a six-game ban was made? Are we to believe he sat there and said nothing to the other people?

"Neil Lennon should have been treated in the same way as any other manager under the SFA procedures. Clearly, that was not the case. It was another spectacular lack of judgmnt from George Peat, and one the club will respond to when Lord Carloway's full report arrives."

Celtic released a statement in response to Lennon's ban being reduced, which read: "Clearly, we are pleased that the Appeals Board has decided to set aside the SFA's original decision in its entirety. We are awaiting the reasons for this in writing and will make further comment when this has been received. The new sanction imposed by the Appeals Board is accepted."

But when they are given the full findings, Celtic are bound to demand why Peat -- who has been involved in verbal spats with the Parkhead club over the past few months -- chose to act as he did. Herald Sport understands that could lead to a claim that his position is now untenable, even though he is into the final few months of his term in office.

George Peat was another type who was a stickler for the rules, unless it came to hurting Celtic.

And Hugh Dallas? Well, he recently pissed off most of Greece and still is talked about in glowing terms by most in the Scottish game. Jim Gannon, ex Motherwell manager who openly criticised Hugh for lying in an exchange with him was rounded upon by celebrity Motherwell fan, Tam Cowan, for daring to question "A man like Hugh Dallas"

Quite.

One last thing, on the night of the famous Hugh Dallas (Bonkle) game at Celtic Park, George Cumming (Carluke) was quoted as saying "Hugh's performance was magnificent today and he proved that he is one of the top referees in Europe. He was under tremendous pressure, and he undoubtedly increased his stature in the game"

Quite.

A Fish Rots From the Head Down

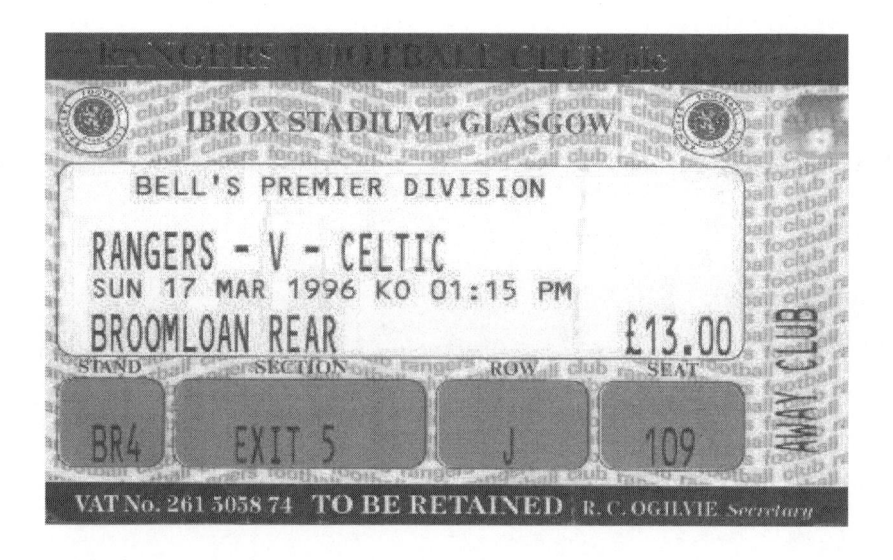

Thursday, May 27th, 1999, 11am. Hampden Park, Glasgow. A wind up is underway. The meeting is regarding the forthcoming Scottish Cup Final between Celtic and Rangers. The previous time a Celtic delegation had met their Rangers counterparts, discussing the upcoming Celtic versus Rangers league game at Celtic Park. At this meeting one of the Rangers party had been badmouthing Manchester United "Joke club, never as big as us, kidding themselves on"

At this meeting for the cup final, it had come a day after Manchester United had completed the treble of European Cup, Premier League and FA Cup.

One of the Celtic delegation noticed an old Manchester United tie in the wardrobe on the morning of the meeting, given to him as part of a gift box at Old Trafford, and saw a gag bubbling under.

Striding into Hampden that day, Red Devil prominent, he knew his Rangers counterpart wouldn't be over the moon at his attire.

As they sat down, the tie was noticed "What the fuck is that?!?!" and a series of expletives came from the Rangers guy's mouth so shocking that he had be told to calm down before they could proceed with the meeting.

Who was the Rangers guy so red at the Red Devil?

Campbell Ogilvie.

More of him later.

If you want a window into how Scottish football works, get George Fulston to open it.

This man, who says his passions are line-dancing and cowboy movies, has long held an enormous hatred of Celtic. With a son who has stood for the Scottish Unionist Party (the same party Mark Dingwall of Follow Follow held the post of Press officer for) you know what you're dealing with. A man who almost single-handedly ran Falkirk and Hamilton into the ground, sat on the SFA committee for years trying and a lot of times succeeding in hindering Celtic at every opportunity. A regular at Ibrox, his favourite haunt was the Lord Nelson pub, where a Celtic employee who had been in the same SFA meeting on the Friday, witnessed the bold George appearing from it, before a 2-0 loss for Celtic at Ibrox in 1997, wearing a Union flag bowler hat.

After investing in a Radio station, the invite list made interesting reading when a certain Nick Griffin, shan yakked nazi former leader of the BNP, was invited to take part in a discussion programme on the station.

Yet George Fulston held enormous power in Scottish football. Using positions at Hamilton and Falkirk, he lobbied well in the lower leagues and got himself on committees within football, the league and the SFA. Like many in the past such as David Will and, of course, George Peat, he used lower league clubs to get top tier status. What did he do with the top tier status? Everything and anything to hinder Celtic. He lobbied hard against Jack McGinn getting the presidency of the SFA, he was instrumental in ensuring Celtic would have to pay top whack to rent out Hampden and he showed consistent and callous contempt when dealing with anyone from Celtic. Yet the media showered him with praise constantly.

Now out the game, he runs Wellman Cars in Hamilton. A massive union flag flies above their depot.

(There ain't no craic in the Union Jack)

*

Campbell Ogilvie is the President of the Scottish Football Association and a former director of Rangers Football Club as well as the former managing director of Scottish Premier League football club Heart of Midlothian.

Ogilvie was appointed assistant secretary of the Scottish Football League in May 1970. In 1978, he was hired as general secretary at Rangers F.C. and in 1989 he became a director of that club. Ogilvie relinquished his executive duties at Ibrox Stadium in September 2005, following a boardroom re-shuffle.

Ogilvie joined Heart of Midlothian in November 2005 to undertake similar duties under the title "Operations Director". Ogilvie was later promoted to managing director on 14 March 2008. Ogilvie held 3505 shares in Rangers FC while a senior manager at Hearts.

In June 2003, Ogilvie became the treasurer, now second vice-president, of the Scottish Football Association (SFA). On 1 June 2007, Ogilvie became first vice-president of the SFA, with Alan McRae taking his place as second vice-president. On 8 June 2011 it was confirmed that Ogilvie would take up the presidency of the Scottish Football Association, succeeding George Peat. (The previous chapter mentions Peat of course)

In March 2012 Ogilvie admitted to being a member of the Employee Benefit Trust scheme at Rangers when he was both a Director of Rangers as well as the treasurer of the Scottish Football Association.

Campbell Ogilvie admits he was 'aware' of Rangers EBT scheme but had no role in player contracts

Campbell Ogilvie has vowed to continue in his role as Scottish Football Association president as he insisted he had no role in "drafting or administering" player contracts at Rangers after the mid-1990s.

The former Rangers company secretary confirmed he had been a member of the Employee Benefit Trust (EBT) scheme, which was the subject of a tax tribunal in January and could cost the Ibrox club £49 million.

Ogilvie moved to clarify his role at the club and insisted he would "look forward to new and exciting challenges ahead at the Scottish FA".

Ogilvie, who was employed at Ibrox from 1978 until leaving for Hearts in 2005, spoke out after his position was questioned given the ongoing investigation into Rangers' financial affairs.

Ogilvie protested his innocence over the contracts issue although he admitted benefiting from the controversial EBT scheme.

In a statement published on the SFA's website, Ogilvie said: "In light of today's comments by (former Rangers owner) Sir David Murray, and the ongoing speculation surrounding my role as president of the Scottish FA and my previous employment as a director of Rangers FC, I would like to take this opportunity to clarify the following points.

"I was aware of the EBT scheme in operation at Rangers during my time at the club and, indeed, was a member. The existence of the scheme was published in Rangers' annual accounts.

"My role at Rangers, until the mid-90s, included finalising the paperwork for player registrations.

"As confirmed by Sir David Murray today, it was never my role to negotiate contracts during my time at Rangers.

"It is also worth noting that, since the mid-90s, I was not responsible for the drafting or administering of player contracts.

"I ceased being company secretary in 2002 and became general secretary responsible for football strategy, in effect becoming the main point of contact between the club and the respective league and governing bodies.

"In relation to the recent investigation, I can confirm that I asked to be excluded from the Scottish FA's independent inquiry into Rangers.

"In the interests of good governance it was absolutely right that this was the case."

The SFA's recent inquiry into Rangers briefly incorporated allegations of undisclosed payments to players following claims by former Ibrox director Hugh Adam.

Adam claimed some payments were not included in official contracts that were registered with the football authorities, with the 86-year-old "pretty sure" similar payments were being made as early as the mid-1990s.

The EBT scheme ran from 2001 to 2010 and followed a similar offshore payments programme from 1999-2003, which sparked a separate £2.8 million claim from Her Majesty's Revenue and Customs. Rangers last year conceded this case but Craig Whyte did not pay the sum after taking over in May.

The SFA dropped their investigations into the issue after the SPL announced an inquiry into the alleged non-disclosure of payments to players from 1998, although the main governing body would hear any appeal.

Ogilvie is determined to carry on in his role, which he was elected to in June last year following a spell as vice-president.

"I am proud and privileged to be president of the Scottish FA during an exciting period in its history," he said.

"I have an excellent relationship with our chief executive, Stewart Regan, and the board of directors.

"I would like to thank them for their support throughout this process and look forward to new and exciting challenges ahead at the Scottish FA."

We also know Stewart Regan backed Campbell Ogilvie on this.

EveningTimes

Regan backs Ogilvie over EBT payout

SFA chief Stewart Regan has defended president Campbell Ogilvie after it emerged that he profited from Rangers' controversial EBT scheme.

There have been calls for the former Rangers secretary to step down from his position in light of his involvement in the practise which is the subject of an SPL investigation and could eventually be referred to the SFA.

But Regan believes Ogilvie has acted completely professionally and insists he has informed the SFA board of his involvement with the payment scheme.

He said: "The president has actually declared what his involvement was as far as player contracts was concerned.

"And we have got very clear feedback that the president was not involved in any letter or correspondence with regards to player EBTs.

"We are all aware of businesses being run where you have one owner and operator running the club and a number of directors sitting below. The way this process has been managed, a lot of this correspondence was done much higher up the chain than Campbell Ogilvie.

"He has been fully up front with the SFA board in terms of his involvement. We are satisfied at the moment that this is not an issue for the board to act on."

Ogilvie actually detailed every piece of information he had available on the EBT scheme from his time at Ibrox and Regan says he has been 100% honest.

"That is why we have asked Campbell, at the outset, to disclose the facts," said Regan.

"That is why Campbell himself asked to be removed from any decision-making and any meeting involving Rangers FC.

"Since February 14 he has had no involvement at all in any board meetings, any decisions or any meetings with the club.

"There has been no involvement from him and, as far as we are concerned, he has done everything he could do to separate himself away from this issue. Let's not forget that EBTs are not illegal.

"They are illegal if they are used knowingly in an incorrect manner. That is something we are still waiting for facts on. But I am satisfied that Campbell has discharged his duty of care.

"He has done everything we could have asked of him and, so far as his integrity is concerned, he is a man with many years as a highly- respected administrator across the game of football in Scotland.

"He has been upfront, transparent and the board are happy we could not have expected any more of him."

166

But we also know both are lying.

THE RANGERS FOOTBALL CLUB plc
Founded 1873

DJO/sh

3 September 1999

The Secretary
Montreal Limited
PO Box 264
Union House
Union Street
St. Helier
Jersey JE4 8TQ

Dear Sir,

On behalf of Rangers Football Club plc I hereby subscribe for two £1 shares in Montreal Ltd at a subscription price of £2 and a share premium of £149,998.

The purpose of this subscription is to provide remuneration to a valued employee of Rangers Football Club plc.

Yours faithfully,

R. C. OGILVIE
SECRETARY/DIRECTOR

MINUTES OF MEETING OF THE BOARD OF DIRECTORS
OF THE RANGERS FOOTBALL CLUB PLC
HELD AT IBROX STADIUM, GLASGOW
ON 16 SEPTEMBER 1999 AT 10.30 AM.

PRESENT: D. E. Murray   Chairman
                R. C. Ogilvie   Secretary
                J. MacDonald

APOLOGIES: H. Adam
                D. Levy
                I. Skelly

IN ATTENDANCE: D. Odam   Financial Controller

Business

The meeting was arranged to consider remuneration planning for the company's employees.

The meeting noted that the company had subscribed for two £1 shares in Montreal Limited.

It was reported that HLB Kidsons had provided advice on remuneration strategy and arrangements designed to incentivise and motivate key employees.

It was resolved to offer the beneficial ownership of the company's shareholding in Montreal Limited as a constituent part of the remuneration package for Craig Moore.

It was the Boards view that the strategy would motivate and incentivise Craig Moore in recognition of his services to Rangers Football Club plc.

There being no further business the Chairman closed the meeting.

AIB Jersey

Private Client

AIBJerseytrust Limited
AIB House
25 Esplanade
St Helier
Jersey
JE1 2AB

Tel: +44 (0) 1534 883000
Fax: +44 (0) 1534 883112
Website: www.aib.je

Our ref: 155/1854760_1.DOC

8th September 2011

STRICTLY PRIVATE & CONFIDENTIAL
The Board of Directors
Rangers Football Club plc
Ibrox Stadium
150 Edmiston Drive
Glasgow
G51 2XD

Telephone: 01534 883000

By recorded delivery

Dear Sirs

Rangers Football Club plc
Montreal Limited
AIBJerseytrust Limited

In September 1999, Mr Ogilvie acting on behalf of Rangers Football Club plc ("Rangers") subscribed for the entire issued share capital of a Manx company, Montreal Limited ("Montreal"), to provide remuneration to one of its players, Mr Moore. We enclose a copy of this letter together with a copy of the minutes of a meeting of Rangers dated 16th September 1999 in which the board resolved to offer the beneficial ownership of Montreal to Mr Moore.

Since its incorporation, Montreal has been administered by AIBJerseytrust Limited ("AIBJ") which is ultimately a wholly owned subsidiary of Allied Irish Banks, p.l.c. The professional fees charged by AIBJ for the provision of directors, secretary and registered office for Montreal together with administration fees for work undertaken have always been settled by Rangers.

On 27th July 2004, my colleague Mr Matthews accompanied by a former director of AIBJ, Mrs Luxo, met with Messrs Olverman and MacMillan in Glasgow, both employees of Rangers or its holding company, Murray International Holdings Limited, to discuss Montreal and other entities under our trusteeship / management including the Rangers Football Club plc EBT ("the EBT"). The minutes of the meeting explain that EBT funds should be used to settle fees relating to Montreal.

A further meeting took place at our offices in Jersey on 16th February 2006 between Mr Matthews, Dr Boon, Mr Carney and Miss Warner, all employees of AIBJ. The meeting had been called by Mr MacMillan to discuss the termination of the EBT and in relation to this, the fourth paragraph of the minutes state *"IM [Mr MacMillan] confirmed that Rangers would continue to pay these fees [Montreal]."*

Since 2009, the fees for Montreal have remained unpaid pending agreement by all parties to the termination of Montreal. On 23rd April 2010, Mr Matthews spoke with Mr MacMillan who confirmed that once the dissolution of Montreal had been agreed with Mr Moore and his advisors, Rangers would release the payment for fees owed to AIBJ in relation to Montreal. This conversation was recorded and a transcript will be prepared if necessary.

1854760-1

AIB Jersey is the registered business name of AIB Bank (CI) Limited and AIBJerseytrust Limited which are regulated by the Jersey Financial Services Commission. AIBJerseytrust Limited is a wholly owned subsidiary of AIB Bank (CI) Limited, which is a wholly owned subsidiary of Allied Irish Banks, p.l.c. The registered office of the above Jersey companies is AIB House, 25 Esplanade, St Helier, Jersey JE1 2AB.

169

There is a paradox with Campbell Ogilvie. Very few people inside Scottish football have a bad word to say about him. Indeed, everyone I spoke to said he is a nice, charming man who was happy to help anyone. Even when he could stick the boot in and was being poked by less rounded human beings at Ibrox, people say he never took the opportunity. Indeed I've spoken to four or five people within Scottish football, including employees of Celtic, who dealt with Ogilvie for many years and all said he was a helpful, friendly guy. One instance of this was when Celtic drew Rangers in the quarter final of the Scottish Cup in 1997. Rangers were entitled to 20% of the then 50,000 capacity of Celtic Park which would have been over 2000 more than their usual allocation. Virtually all in high positions pushed and shoved Campbell Ogilvie to get the 10,000 tickets they were entitled to but Campbell took the view that the shoe would be on the other foot one day and agreed with Celtic to take the normal Rangers allocation, much to the chagrin of others at Rangers.

On another occasion, an employee of a football club was asked to go to a SPL meeting to represent his club on an issue that was going a lot of angst for the likes of Rod Petrie at Hibs and Chris Robinson at Hearts and the employee was nervous, he'd never been at one of these meetings before and was simply filling in for someone else. Campbell Ogilvie noticed his nerves, took him aside and told he would be fine, he knew his stuff and there was nothing to worry about.

Don't get me wrong here, I would have loved nothing more, for the purposes of this book, if the folk I spoke to about Campbell Ogilvie all said "Oh him aye, what a right bastard he is" but they didn't. So this does beg the question: Why did Campbell Ogilvie end up in such a mess with the EBT scheme and have his reputation and credibility completely ruined?

I asked this question of all I spoke to who knew him and all had a long think before coming to roughly the same conclusion: David Murray.

I have pretty much said as much anyone on David Murray and the conclusion I come to is that Murray clearly had something on Campbell Ogilvie. Remember that, as well as being pretty much the most powerful man in Scotland, David Murray was untouchable in Scottish football and held a big sway within UEFA, playing a role in the beginning of the Champions League, and he could do a hell of a lot for the likes of Campbell Ogilvie. He could also take it all away. I don't know what Murray had on Ogilvie but Ogilvie has danced to his tune for decades now and never dropped a dime once. That tells its own story.

*

Jim Ballantyne was a fanatical Rangers supporter despite coming from a family of Airdrie supporters. When Rangers died and Sevco formed a Newco, Jim decided to support them as well. As a youngster, Jim was known around Stepps as Jimmy and then "Jimmy1690" given his fanatical devotion to all things loyalist. Indeed he even had a Union Flag bedspread. His sister Anne (real name Anne-Marie) is an Airdrie supporter. The family business was an accountancy firm in St Enoch's square and whilst the family were building that business, Jimmy1690 was a regular attender at Ibrox with his friends Colin Logan, Dougie Kennedy and Andy Watt to name but three.

When the chance to buy New Airdrie came around, Jimmy1690 jumped at it and Anne-Marie was glad she had dropped the Marie from her name when she took over the day to day running of the club.

This allowed Jimmy1690 to take over the George Fulston role of being one of the best lobbyists in the game. So much so that even though the SPL had split away from the Scottish Football League Jimmy1690 became a powerful figure in Scottish football. So much so that when David Longmuir became the CEO of the Scottish Football League, he only answered to one guy and that was our friend Jimmy1690.

Change was in the air by then. Everyone knew Rangers were heading for liquidation and the SPL and Scottish Football League were heading for merger. This was a nightmare for Jimmy1690. As well as owning Airdrie, he had shares in Rangers and knew his power would be eroded by the merger. When it came to a shoot-out between Neil Doncaster and David Longmuir for the gig of CEO of the newly formed SPFL, Jimmy1690 lobbied hard for his man to get the gig but couldn't match the power of the top dogs in the top league and Longmuir was out. Just before the interview process began, David Longmuir's contract had a three month termination clause on it. In other words, in the event of losing that job, he would get three month's salary. The day before his interview, that clause became 12 months.

I'm guessing you've worked out who changed that contract.

*

What of our own leaders? I think it is only fair that I look at the two main ones of the last 20 years and the guy being groomed to be the next one. Fergus is analysed in a future chapter but "Gas Meter" is right now. I don't think you need me to go on about Peter Lawwell's career, you all know it, but I think, given the perception of Peter Lawwell from a lot of the media and virtually everyone who doesn't support Celtic, it's only fair that I try to find out if he is the master manipulator he is made out to be and therefore, perhaps, gives an excuse for an anyone but Celtic attitude of others to continue. I've criticised Peter Lawwell on many occasions. He's not daft, he knows this. It's never been done out of anything personal or a desire to be negative, simply for the purpose of wanting Celtic to be bigger, stronger and faster. My first encounter with him was in July 2006. I was asked by John Paul Taylor to assemble a few bloggers, website guys and so on for a meeting with Peter Lawwell. No reason was given why. Once in the meeting, in an upstairs room at Celtic Park, it was obvious what Lawwell wanted. Ahead of a visit to Tynecastle, he wanted all of us on board regarding a statement he was going to put out regarding the singing of rebel songs. Some of us in the room were very sceptical whilst others jumped on board immediately. I didn't say much in the meeting but afterwards went for a pint with Average Joe Miller and we both agreed that this wasn't really for us. I've sang rebel songs all my life and there was no way I was going to help push a statement urging others to stop singing them. Whatever anyone thinks, rebel songs have been part of Celtic fan culture for at least 100 years and there has to be a real debate before anything can be decided. This is what I relayed to Peter Lawwell and JPT and that was the end of me at the meetings.

Due to where I was living (New York) not long after that, this wasn't really an issue but there was a definite disconnect between me and certain people at Celtic and when JPT left in 2008, I assumed that would be my last contact with anyone at Celtic outside the ticket office.

Then I arrived back in Scotland for a while and took a phone call one day asking if I wanted to go to the press conference that would announce Tony Mowbray as new manager. I turned it down. Not out of any principled stance, pig-headedness or otherwise. Quite simply, I was skint.

I went back to New York until 2012 and had little contact with Celtic outside the sort anyone would have.

Again, I thought that was it until I was emailing with JPT one day in May 2013 and, as his wont, he sent a cryptic message that hinted he was coming back to Celtic. Initially I thought tickets but as we all know it was to be the new Supporters Liaison Officer.

This meant, down the line, contact again with Peter Lawwell and myself.

That's not a big thing and is not intended to sound so, it's merely to provide some sort of context as to why my views on Peter Lawwell changed over the years. I had been both critical and sceptical of what he was doing at Celtic. For years I couldn't see anything other than a downsizing of quality at the club. Stories emerged of underhand dealings and specific targeting of certain fans and an ever increasing disconnect between Lawwell and the fans grew bigger. It was at this point when JPT dropped the dime to say he was coming back.

If you think I am about say "And we all lived happily ever after" you're wrong.

I was for an SLO at Celtic and no one on this planet or any other is more qualified for the role than JPT. For me, and many others, the supporters are Celtic and always will be. So to have a liaison to, well, liaise with is a great idea. However, I don't think JPT knew the scale of the widening disconnect between a lot of fans and the club when he took over the role in July 2013. I think it's fair to say that his first year in the job was tough and guys like me ensured that. Not because we wanted to but because we had so many issues with the way things were being run. Often I would have serious, heated arguments with JPT about the direction the club was taking or even just the way a fan had been treated by a member of staff. I can honestly our relationship fractured a bit at times and this was a solid 20 year friendship I am talking about here. However, things started to get better and slowly things started to happen. The Green Brigade were finally treated like adults and with respect and the club started to appreciate the pressure being put on these guys by the authorities. I was there that day the Green Brigade were "kettled" just off the Gallowgate and the only time I've seen the police act that way in public had been at Republican marches. It was outrageous what happened that day.

Thankfully JPT grasped the nettle and a much better, at the time of writing, relationship between the club and Green Brigade has blossomed.

Similarly, fan-club relations are much better. They aren't perfect by any means but I think we have now reached a point where fans and club both understand where each other are coming from. JPT has moulded the SLO role into his own. I believe that will be a CEO role in the future. It was also JPT that ensured that I had conversations with Peter Lawwell again and in one, my opinion changed of the man.

I'd been pushing and pushing for Peter Lawwell to say something publicly on the "same club" horseshit that had filled the airwaves and columns of our press. His argument was that if he did, he would light a fuse that would ultimately end up with someone being hurt or even killed, mine was that no matter what he said, the other mob would never hate him any less. Don't get me wrong, I can appreciate his argument and have argued all the way through this book about the ugly side of Scottish society. It was at a later date that Lawwell floored me a bit.

Chris White, he of "old board" infamy, loved Celtic. I know that can be read many ways and even more arguments can go against that statement but the point is he loved Celtic from the time of being a wee boy. The other point is, because of his public persona, he feels now that he can't go back to Celtic games, ever, and that has broken him. Unlike Michael Kelly, he's never said anything publicly and shunned the media ever since 1994.

I'm not here trying to detoxify Chris White, I'm leading you into the argument, if you can call it that, Peter Lawwell gave me in May 2015. He talked about how his wife and family went to the games, his own family were all season ticket holders. He said that if he ever did anything to besmirch Celtic then not only would he be finished with the club but so to would his family and that would kill him. This was a side of Peter Lawwell I'd never seen before and I'll be honest here, it got me. I can be one of the world's most stubborn people when it comes to standing my ground on things and can often forget the human factor and this brought it home to me a bit. Whatever anyone thinks of Peter Lawwell's decisions, I don't believe the man would intentionally expose Celtic in any way.

Unlike pretty much anyone who has ran the game in Scotland or held any position of power in the game.

*

The worrying thing about all these types, the ones who appear and suddenly have offices at Hampden, is their total lack of self-awareness. When I was finishing this chapter the FIFA scandal broke and Stewart Regan decided to sum that lack up perfectly.

Stewart Regan has today reiterated the Scottish FA's call for change within FIFA, world football's governing body.

Following today's revelations in Zurich ahead of Friday's FIFA Congress, the Chief Executive revealed that should the Presidential election go ahead as planned, the Scottish FA would vote for Prince Ali bin al-Hussein, the only standing opponent to FIFA President Sepp Blatter, after the withdrawals of Dutch FA President, Michael van Praag, and the Portuguese legend, Luis Figo, last week.

The Chief Executive, the President, Campbell Ogilvie, and vice-President, Alan McRae, flew out to Zurich today ahead of the FIFA Congress, which is now shrouded in uncertainty and controversy after a number of FIFA officials were arrested. The Scottish FA delegation will attend a meeting with UEFA, European football's governing body, and its 54 member associations ahead of the Congress.

"What has happened today underlines the need for fundamental change in how FIFA is governed," said Regan. "We will discuss the

Scottish FA's position with UEFA but also establish the position of all European national associations when we receive more information on what is a developing situation.

"We have stated before that we believe for the good of the game's image, integrity and indeed future prosperity that Mr Blatter should stand down and allow FIFA to radically improve its governance and credibility. After today's events, that position has crystallised still further."

You do wonder if Regan laughed as he said that.

That's why we're paranoid

Ally Morrison
@ally_morrison

Off to Ibrox to see Greg referee his first Rangers game. Do the Ayrshire association proud and gee us three points big man!

1:30 PM · 22 Feb 14

May 21st, 2005, 3.46pm, Fir Park, Motherwell. Scott McDonald has just scored his second goal in a meaningless match for Motherwell but an enormous one for Celtic. The tension had been fraught since the morning of the game with a pressure cooker like build up started with morning headlines that Celtic manager, Martin O'Neill, was to stand down to take care of his ill wife and Gordon Strachan was to take over. Celtic supporters had basked under the O'Neill leadership and, speaking personally, it felt like a death in the family.

The title scenario was pretty straightforward, beat Motherwell at Fir Park and Celtic were Champions. Anything less than that would mean that a Rangers win at Easter Road would see them take the league title.

The tension in the air was palpable. Celtic would have had the title wrapped up before the day were not for an uncharacteristic defeat at home to a Hibs team which was in a period of prosperity of producing its own players and the young legs were too much for an ageing and weary Celtic team to cope with in a deserved 3-1 loss.

A 2-0 win over Aberdeen at Celtic Park the following week steadied the ship and was followed up with a hard fought 2-1 win at Tynecastle where, ironically, three future Celtic players (Gordon, Pressley and Hartley) did everything they could to stop Celtic winning, Gordon going up for a corner in the final minute, Pressley diving in the box in the final minute and Hartley equalising a Thompson goal in the 71st minute.

The morning of the final league game of the season, Celtic fans awoke to the news that Gordon Strachan would be the man to replace Martin O'Neill as manager. The thought process of the vast majority of Celtic fans would be to win the league and worry about it later.

The game itself was tense, played in that grey but warm kind of weather that always seems to engulf Lanarkshire at that time of year. Chris Sutton cooled the air slightly with a 29th minute opener but most in the stadium knew this Celtic team was flailing towards an iceberg. Chances were spurned, arguments raged and nails were bitten more than a fresh apple. Yet it looked like Celtic would fall over the line right until the 88th minute when Scott McDonald hooked a shot into the top corner and put the league into the hands of Rangers. A stunned anger washed over the Celtic end of Fir Park like a sudden tsunami. Chris Sutton tried to score immediately from kick off but it was in vain and the shock allowed McDonald to dance up the pitch and loop another one in to send most of Scotland into raptures.

At that minute, a prominent Celtic official could watch no more and made their way to the boardroom to try and comprehend what had just happened. As they approached the door they saw two Motherwell directors shaking champagne, like a Grand Prix winner, and shouting "Ya fucking beauty!!!!"

Anyone but Celtic.

One of the hardest parts of writing this book has been that in the time I was writing it, the raft of material just kept building and building as honest mistakes and SFA bias came as frequently as *Coronation Street.*

Week after week I'd get tweets saying "another chapter for the book, Paul" any time I tried to highlight yet another farce brought to you by the people who run the game in Scotland.

To Celtic supporters, it appears as though we face so many baffling decisions that the rest of the country has become immune to it, aside from this who use them as a stick to beat the club with. Looking at the most recent example of a horrendous decision against Celtic, the Josh Meekings handball at Hampden, the usual pattern emerged. The initial reporting of the incident was just that, reporting. The referee's observer report was submitted, as normal, that night and it said that Alan Muir, the goal line referee had seen the incident and said it hit Meekings on the face. Whilst most observers thought TV showed him shouting "Hand, Hand, Hand", he claimed he was shouting "Head, Head, Head". By the following day that report had changed, why? Well, on the Monday, Celtic wrote to the SFA and asked for clarification on the decision not to award a penalty. The SFA wrote back saying no officials had seen the incident and that's why the penalty wasn't given.

The media reporting of the incident also followed a familiar pattern. Most outlets reported the incident and the obvious wrong decision but within 24 hours the pundits and columnist were all over it and the usual "paranoid Celtic" narrative was created.

Not for the first time.

My bug bear on this is that Celtic get worried that this casts a negative shadow on that club. They will say "Any time we challenge a decision, we get hit with "paranoid Celtic". I see that and it has become similar to the Tory conditioning of "Labour can't run the economy" of the electorate in the UK. Yet it is no reason to back down. I've said it before and I'll say it again, nothing we say or do will ever make them hate us any less.

I can go back 25 years when Paul Elliot, a phenomenal centre half in his two years at Celtic, was booked 14 times in a row at one point in his Celtic career. The media started a campaign to justify this by claiming Elliot was overly aggressive and one even claimed that he "didn't know how to handle Dougie Arnott". This is a guy who had successfully man marked Diego Maradona when playing for Pisa against Napoli in a 0-0 draw in them Serie A.

Around the same time, Celtic went an entire year without getting a penalty in Scotland. It became a running joke with my friends at the time, in the days where a wireless or Pink News was your only chance of getting information from other games in Scotland (particularly if you were at a game yourself) and I would get asked, upon returning from the Celtic game, "Did you get a penalty the day then?". The media, once again, had the answer "Celtic don't get in the box enough, that's the problem" Yet for the bulk of the season that Celtic were not given a penalty, they had three strikers who were scoring goals all the time. Gerry Creaney, Tommy Coyne and Charlie Nicholas all hit over 20 goals that season and I can assure you most of them were from inside the box.

At the time of writing, Celtic have won the last four league Championships. No Celtic manager has been awarded the manager of the year. The reason given, usually inflated by the media, is "More money than everyone else". It is interesting therefore that when Rangers "won" nine championships in a row their manager won the award seven out of the nine seasons with only Andy Roxburgh (Scotland) and Alex Totten (St Johnstone) denying them a clean sweep.

There was a draw for the League Cup semi-finals in 1993 that had Celtic, Rangers, Hibs and Dundee Utd taking part. The draw would be made at Ibrox, directly after Rangers had beaten Aberdeen 2-1 after extra time. Representing Celtic at the draw was Joe Jordan. For Rangers it was Walter Smith. At the time, Hampden was being, I want to say re-developed but was it really? So if Celtic and Rangers were drawn together they would be tossing a coin to see who would host the game. The inevitable happened and the coin toss was organised. Joe Jordan called tails and tails it was. Happy days for Celtic. Joe started to speak about how delighted he was that the game would be at Celtic Park when someone interrupted him and said "That was just to see who would be calling" and a nation, watching live on TV, gasped. The coin was thrown again, Joe called tails again and it was heads. The game would be played at Ibrox.

Then there was Rod McDonald.

A Scouser, he was booked as he went off the park at half time for blessing himself after scoring a goal for Partick Thistle against Rangers.

The player was later booked for a tackle against John Brown and was dismissed. McDonald and the team manager, Murdo MacLeod, were called to the referee's room during the interval and it was pointed out that the police had been alerted by some Rangers fans who saw the player make his gesture. The police took no action, but the referee did, although McDonald appeared unaware he had been cautioned. When Jim McGilvray booked him for his challenge on the Rangers player McDonald turned away as though to continue playing and then looked surprised when he realised he had to leave the pitch. It seems McDonald may have blessed

185

himself after he scored his goal, but it was an action which could lead to his suspension. Presumably the referee, who missed one or two other incidents, felt the player's gesture might have incited some trouble among Rangers' support, but Murdo MacLeod and his chairman took a different view. "Rod blesses himself as he goes on and off the pitch in every game," the manager said. "He does it in reserve matches also. "I've never seen anyone in Italy, for instance, being cautioned for doing that and so far as Rod is concerned it is normal practice for him. It's at times like this you know which city you are in.".

Partick Thistle chairman, Jim Oliver, said "I understand that after he scored the goal he crossed himself" Oliver said, "and I don't think he realised that constituted a yellow card. If he was being booked for his action after his goal then he should have been cautioned at that time, in 35 minutes, and not 10 minutes later. Why this should constitute a foul in football is beyond me, but because we have the Rangers' situation here it seems a different set of rules are invoked. 'I have to be guarded about what I say, but it is ridiculous" Thistle had another player, Billy McDonald, dismissed in the final minutes after he had become involved in an exchange with Paul Gascoigne, who scored both Rangers' goals. The pair had tussled on a few occasions during the game and in fact, both should have been punished just after the interval when they came together in a flurry of arms and legs. McGilvray took no action at all, when quite clearly he should have. It makes you wonder if he realised that by booking McDonald or worse, by sending him off, Gascoigne, too, would have deserved a yellow card at least. The Rangers player had already been booked for having celebrated his first goal by leaping an advertising board. In booking Gascoigne for that the referee was seen as churlish and officious and the later incident left McGilvray open to question. "There were implications in that instance," was all Oliver was willing to say.

And on it goes.

Steve McLean models 'Celtic penalty' pose.

I watched the Inverness Semi-Final in Perth, WA. The welcome I got from the likes of Andy Gordon, Davy Barclay and Paddy McOnie will live long in the memory. As will what I witnessed on the big screen on a Sunday night in Rosie O'Grady's. I talked to my good friend, Frank Rafters of Maley's Bhoys, and felt his cool head was needed to summarise that day:

"On the nineteenth of April 2015, I passed through the turnstiles into the North Stand of Hampden Park with a blend of assurance and apprehension in my mind. Now twenty-five years of age, I have only ever seen Celtic win the treble once, and that was a little shy of my eleventh birthday, so the enormity of upcoming tie with Inverness Caledonian Thistle was abruptly clear to me. My confidence came, predominantly, from the influence of Ronny Deila. He had brought his team a long way from the woes of Warsaw and had already secured the Scottish League Cup in some style. However, the sources of my nerves were two-fold. Firstly, Celtic always have the potential to perform poorly at Hampden, often when you least expect it, and secondly, my gut told me to be wary of those officiating the tie. Sadly, despite a bright start ignited by a thunderous free-kick from Virgil van Dijk, both of the previously referenced factors which contributed to my prior unease would come to the fore.

Midway through the first half, with the Celts already a goal ahead, Stefan Johansen's shot was saved by Ryan Esson, before the rebound was headed goal wards by Leigh Griffiths. Between the Celtic striker and the goalmouth stood Josh Meekings, who raised his outstretched right arm away from his body and produced a save of which any goalkeeper would have been proud.

Now, anyone who watches Celtic regularly will know that there are three distinctly different crowd reactions which accompany potential penalty shouts. There is the award for which a very small percentage of the fans claim, whilst the majority remain unmoved. Such appeals can, on occasion, be exacerbated if the team is in desperate need of a goal, but even then these are often made in forlorn hope rather than serious expectation. Next, there is the appeal which splits the support fairly evenly, with perhaps half the crowd claiming for a spot kick whilst the others express their suspicion that there was no infringement. These situations may often be followed by people lamenting their desire "to see that one again" on a television screen. Lastly, and most spectacularly, there is the instantaneous, unanimous roar. In this situation, no time is taken to consider the matter – people simply respond instinctively to that which they have seen. Reactions such as this are raw and, more often than not, correct.

Unsurprisingly, the response which followed Josh Meekings' handball fell into the last of these categories. Upon the occurrence of the incident, all of those sitting around me, who had been fairly sedate until that point, leapt to their feet as one, screaming for a penalty kick. This cacophony of noise continued as everyone – Josh Meekings included, as he reared his head back in despair – expected referee Steven McLean to point to the spot. However, as the seconds passed, it became clear to everyone that no penalty would be awarded. An inevitable torrent of jeers then followed, as the collective mood within the Celtic support altered from that of quiet optimism to one of intense distrust.

Subsequently, as Craig Gordon and Marley Watkins collided in the second half, there was no doubt in the majority of people's minds that a red card and spot kick would be awarded, ironically in the same penalty box which saw the Celts' earlier claims denied. Thereafter, it would be an uphill battle for Celtic, with goals from Edward Ofere and David Raven, tempered only by a free kick from

John Guidetti, ultimately sending the Hoops out of the competition.

As I trudged away from the National Stadium following the final whistle, comments such as "we were screwed" were easily audible, and the odd child in tears perhaps personified how we were all feeling. Personally, I believed that I had witnessed the worst officiating decision of my life, and although I have only been attending Celtic matches since 1997, there have been some awful examples.

Before continuing, allow me to be absolutely clear – whenever Celtic lose, I am naturally disappointed, but defeat is much easier to accept when it has been achieved by our opposition outplaying us rather than through controversy. The Celts did not produce a performance to match their potential that day at Hampden, but that matters for little as had a penalty and sending off followed Meekings' handball as it blatantly should have, the tie would have been all but over. Facing ten men, our chances of progression would have increased (and Inverness' decreased) almost irrevocably, particularly if the ensuing penalty was scored.

Following on from a defeat in the 1893 Scottish Cup Final against Queen's Park (wherein a shot which went wide of the post was given as what transpired to be the winning goal), Celtic lobbied the Scottish Football Association for the introduction of goal nets in future ties and were successful. Nowadays, their use is taken for granted. Therefore, in the modern day, perhaps we should be at the forefront of the push for video technology?

Fundamentally, Celtic were denied an opportunity to play Falkirk not only for the Scottish Cup of 2015 – but for a domestic treble –

by either sheer incompetence of the highest order, or something altogether more sinister. It is not for me to tell you which of these to believe, as I feel the numerous still pictures, video highlights and camera angles do so better than any written words. It is not simply the fact that such decisions are made which troubles me, but that if anyone within the Celtic support – people who pay their hard earned money to watch their team – raise any concerns whatsoever, they are derided by the media and supporters of other sides for having the audacity to ask questions and demand better. We are vilified when it is clear, to any rational individual at least, that we have done nothing wrong.

It's time for accountability; it's time for change; it's time for a level playing field, once and for all"

Image taken from the website of the Lanarkshire Referees Association the week before the Inverness v Celtic semi-final.

Don't Call It a Comeback

The Asterisk Years told of how the Edinburgh Establishment used influence, contacts and privilege to create a world that would allow them to do whatever they wanted, whenever they wanted. When David Murray got to the top of that world what he wanted was to propel Rangers to the top of European football and consign Celtic to the annals of history. Whilst his access to Scotland's banks, judges and limitless off shore trusts were key in this strategy, Murray was fortunate in that there was already one organisation in existence that had a long history of being Anti-Celtic. The SFA's tentacles cover all aspects of Scottish football and whilst Murray was able to control the administrative aspect of the organisation, the boots on the ground were that of the Lanarkshire Referees Association. The context of the story is important. As is the timeline. Murray had tried, and failed, to kill Celtic and a successful takeover from Fergus McCann had seen a complete change in attitude from Celtic, a proper strategy put in place and a change in the banking facilities, first to the Allied Irish and then to the Cooperative Bank, from the previous enemies that the club used ensured Murray's friends at the Bank of Scotland were no longer in control of Celtic's finances.

Similarly though, Celtic's strengthening, which began with Fergus McCann, was and is a huge obstacle to the club's enemies. At the time of re-birth under Fergus, the internet was starting to get bigger also. This enabled the club's followers to realise that there were people in Perth, Western Australia with Celtic hearts as big as those in the Gallowgate. This sharing of passion, worldwide, was the platform upon which the Internet Bampots were born. I spoke about this is in *By Any Means Necessary: Journey with Celtic Bampots.*

It is also important to look back how the club did get bigger, better, faster and stronger back in 1994.

When Fergus took over the club it took some time to really notice the changes. During that period he was busy putting a framework in place that all staff at the club would work to. He also had the issues of who would join him and who wouldn't, so the day to day team at Celtic were largely responsible for keeping things going.

There were some subtle differences at first. There was an emphasis on retaining data, this was never really something Celtic would have considered previously but all of a sudden if someone contacted the Club it was essential they kept their details. Fergus naturally coming from a marketing background understood the value of data but for Celtic it just wasn't something they had thought about.

After this, external agencies were employed to carry out marketing campaigns again a new concept for Celtic. Next were the additional resources coming in and the need to beef up the frontline team. Obviously Fergus was aware that he would be launching a blitz on Celtic fans from around the world and he had a strong belief that there would be a massive response to his call to arms. So within a few months all departments at Celtic were told to staff up which was done through agencies, bringing in dozens of agency workers to help answer telephones, respond to correspondence and deal with supporters face to face. In many respects it was counter-productive as there was no training so it meant in many cases the people just got in the way, gave the wrong information or in some cases lasted all of half an hour before bolting out the door.

Bringing in people from employment agencies meant Celtic were bringing in a different type of person from what they were used to, and the people came across as more professional. Fergus knew this was needed. He wanted high calibre individuals with a university degree who had operated at a senior level. Very much what you would expect nowadays from a top organisation but it was a bit of a culture shock at the time for those at Celtic.

Some of the appointments worked very well whilst some others didn't. The Glasgow football working environment is not for everyone. Salaries remained pretty much as they were as did contracts. Conditions didn't really change either, the big projects were getting somewhere to play whilst the stadium was being constructed, signing players that would challenge the domination experienced from across the city and attracting investment through the Share Offer. On top of that there was a marketing campaign to be assembled for the sale of Season Tickets, a sale the likes of which Celtic had never seen before so anything else was put on the back burner. There was a job to be done and everyone put their shoulder to the wheel, it was about Celtic not individuals so folk just got the head down and got on with it.

Bear in mind though, no one could be sure the investment would come so no one knew if the Club would have the means to keep going. Then there was always the new boss factor, would Fergus be right? Would he rate the staff there? Everyone had to justify themselves in some form or another, Fergus was extremely subtle in how he would go about things but he just went about his business and formed opinions about people and, over time, some stayed, some went, some moved into other roles some moved sideways but it was all done very subtly, no drama, he instinctively knew when someone was right for a position and went about filling the gaps in a quiet and methodical way.

He also despised bullshit. He hated anyone trying to pull the wool over his eyes, he could spot it a mile away and if anyone tried to bullshit him he didn't suffer them gladly at all. He was a straight shooter and detested any form of dishonesty, as Jim Farry would soon realise, he wouldn't tolerate it. He also hated anyone trying to use the Club for their own ends, anyone who tried to ride on the back of Celtic whilst lining their own pocket or if someone was abusing their position or trust, for example to get tickets or access to players, that type of thing. It was a Club, a business and was to be run that way, no inside tracks, no wide boys, everything had to be on the up and up. No one walked away. Obviously there were staff who he valued and trusted but he never acted in a way that it was obvious to anyone. Put it this way, if he didn't like you, you were out, if he didn't trust you, you were out, if he didn't rate you, you were out so if you saw out his reign you must have been doing something right.

Fergus wasn't one for grand speeches, he came in and just got straight to work. A few months previous to him coming in staff had all be called in to the boardroom to be told about the move to Cambuslang and the Gefinor deal but when Fergus came in he did everything in a very quiet and business-like manner. He definitely didn't like a fuss.

Folk who worked under him said he was a brilliant boss, definitely up there with the best they had ever worked with. He would make himself available for people if they needed to speak to him, no matter whether you were a major player in terms of the company structure or not and he would spend time giving anyone the benefit of his experience. He would also tell staff about the work he did in advance of coming in and it was amazing for them to see his plans and how they actually went from a sheet of paper to what we now currently see as Celtic Park. Fergus was a genius and a visionary but very humble. He also had a very good sense of humour. He probably did get angry but no one saw him giving anyone a dressing down in public, he did things properly, he was a real professional.

It took a month or two before staff really seen much of a difference then. The marketing campaign was launched and after that the Club never really looked back. They were being inundated with season ticket requests, phones, counter, mail you name it. They were under siege. Cash was pouring in and people were fighting to get their hands on season tickets. There were fights almost every day as fans queued to buy into the dream. Fergus had woken up a sleeping giant, people who hadn't been to matches for years were all of a sudden turning up and buying in bulk. People weren't buying in ones and twos it was fours and fives and, in the case of supporters clubs, Celtic were seeing orders for forty, fifty and even up to two hundred in some cases. When all of this started to kick in the staff just knew Celtic were on their way to being a force again, people had bought into the vision, the dream to see Celtic back on top, new stadium and no longer the poor relations. Celtic were on their way firing the first arrow at the Murray regime and they knew it. Those weeks and months were pivotal in Celtic's history, the club has never really looked back since then, they were off and running and nothing was going to stop them.

The Hampden season was a bit of a drag, no one would deny that, but it paved the way for what lay ahead, in the summer of 1995,

Celtic returned to a new North Stand and bright vibrant team and manager and the team went on to play some of the best football any of the fans had seen. It would end in disappointment that year, in 1996, but everyone could see that Celtic were back, the construction of the Lisbon Lions stand had begun, they had won the Scottish Cup and were back in Europe. It was only a matter of time before Celtic would regain the title, there was a belief, you knew it was coming, everyone did. Fergus had set Celtic on the path and slowly but surely Celtic just kept progressing, going forward together taking on all comers, beating all sorts of records for ticket sales, season ticket sales, share purchases, to a goal of becoming an unstoppable force.

And David Murray knew this.

The Lanarkshire Referees Association also knew this.

Of course, the other key component in the Celtic revival was Tommy Burns.

Tommy was the perfect manager for Celtic. He grew up on the doorstep, came as a fan, made it as a player, he knew Celtic, he understood Celtic. Tommy had Celtic in his heart, he knew what it meant to the fans, he understood the need to win every game, to be top dog in Glasgow, he knew the priorities, because they were his priorities, to make Celtic the best that they could be.

Tommy was brilliant with staff at Celtic but then Tommy was brilliant with everyone, he always made time for people and never dismissed anyone. Tommy knew everyone at Celtic by name and made sure everyone celebrated in any of the success that the team enjoyed, on the night Celtic won the Scottish Cup in 1995, the first trophy in six years, he made sure everyone was part of the celebration, it was a Celtic party and everyone from top to bottom was part of it. Although he was Celtic manager Tommy could operate at different levels, he could be with the punters in the car park, with the players or with the directors in the boardroom, he knew how to conduct himself and never thought he was better than anyone else, he seen his role as an honour and he respected it.

It was often said that Tommy was "too much of a fan" but that is clearly nonsense, Tommy wanted what the fans wanted, he knew the expectations on Celtic and he gave them the fast flowing, attractive football, as good as anything the fans seen in years. Let's not forget he went through a league season losing only one match, in any other year that would have been enough to win the title. We now know why that happened of course and no one suffered from Rangers cheating more than Tommy Burns. He brought some great players and created a brilliant team, perhaps he was just unfortunate to be manager at the wrong time, but to be Celtic manager was never the wrong time for Tommy, and no one could question his team or the football his teams played, they played the Celtic way, being so close to the Club and the fans Tommy knew what was expected and in almost every aspect he delivered.

In terms of the stress of the job it did begin to tell on him towards the end of that unfortunate league campaign, Celtic so close to the title undone by a series draws that came in a period when they were denied a striker for six weeks. For Tommy there was a really high level of frustration as he knew how important it was to be Champions, he was desperate to clinch the title and, just as important, he knew we were good enough, he just never got that wee bit of luck that every manager needs to get him over the line.

He also had no real idea, like any Celtic fan then, what dark forces were raging against his Celtic.

Tommy's players during that period were excellent, Celtic were just on the cusp of the superstar period but most of the lads at the time still had a real feeling for the Club, Packie Bonner, Paul McStay, John Collins, Tosh McKinlay, Peter Grant, Tom Boyd, Malky McKay, Simon Donnelly, Charlie Nicholas and Frank McAvennie had been in and around at that time and they were all local(ish) lads so no one was ever going to get above themselves with them around. Some of the foreign players included at the time Pierre, Di Canio, Cadete, Vata, Thom and they were all decent guys, Cadete was really quiet and never spoke much but Pierre and Di Canio were always full of fun, they loved being around the Club and they loved the adulation they got from the fans. Let's also say, if we ever needed to, that Di Canio was nuts.

The home based players made sure they were aware of what it meant, no one ever got the impression from any of them that it didn't matter to them. Most were all really decent guys particularly Pierre, Rudi and Andy Thom who were all very popular with all staff at Celtic.

Of course this was the time when tickets really took off and that was no different for the players. As you would expect they always took tickets for the bigger games, especially those at Ibrox although there is no doubt that the home based players would make sure the foreign players took their allocation so they could promptly relieve them of them. It was generally ten per first team player in those days. Most of the home based players bought season tickets, the Club provided a two for one offer and pretty much all the players took up the offer. An encouraging sign for all.

Tommy had a great way of managing the players and there was never really any disharmony within the group, Paul McStay was a great captain and he was a strong character, again he knew the Club and the demands so he set a good example, he had the respect of the players so it was always a happy camp.

With the club on the up, it meant more demands on staff, more demands on players and a different strategy required. Scratch that, a strategy was required. There was no real strategy in the early years. After the takeover the Club went into meltdown in terms of demand for season tickets and match tickets. They did all they could do to try to cope with demand but the truth is, they had very little expertise with dealing with campaigns of that magnitude, they had next to no technology and even if they did they didn't really have any technical expertise, which Fergus had identified and was actively trying to fix. This was a whole new ball game. Things happened so quickly that everything was reactive, Celtic were writing the script as they went in this sense. To be fair the Club recognised this and brought in someone with a bit more experience of managing these type of situations. David McDermott wasn't really a football man as such, but he brought a level of expertise which was badly missing, he was able to take the emotion out things and had a strategic approach so that it helped to bring things under control.

The other problem was the stadium and the dreaded Hampden year which was just so difficult as Celtic didn't know until six weeks prior that they were going, there were no seating plans and finally they just had to put a big stadium map on the wall to let everyone select their preferred location, of course about five thousand people selected the halfway line in the North Stand. There were also the demands put on the club by Jim Farry, a million pounds rent was charged for the season, the club were not allowed to put any Celtic signage at Hampden and, worst of all, they could not fly the Irish tricolour at Hampden. The practical reality was that for every "home" match at Hampden they had to arrange a lorry to pick up a porta cabin which was then set up for match day ticket sales. After these were concluded they had to cash up, get the money away to Securicor then arrange for the porta cabin to be uplifted. It was a horrible time for all staff and fans.

The increased demand in away tickets meant that Celtic were having more and more ballots, those were the days where you sent in your vouchers from your season book, an entire office full of vouchers per game, all boxed up, but they were over-subscribed for almost every match. The ballots were just drawn randomly, there was no loyalty attached so it was effectively just your luck if you got a ticket. This was all well and good until Celtic played at Ibrox, people would send in envelopes which would be a metre square so that they would stand out in the ballot, it really was that basic.
 Also the more vouchers you sent the better chance you had as the team would look for the big numbers to get through their tickets faster, all very unfair but that was the fore runner for the away registration scheme, they knew that things couldn't go on so they worked out a more fair and equitable way of allocating tickets.

In 1993 they had five ticket office staff, this grew steadily and at one point there was a team of 46. This of course presented its own problems, that is a big number to manage and they had to start dividing into sub groups and developing a proper department structure. This was all done on the run whilst keeping everything else running, home games, away games, season tickets, instalment schemes, home cup ticket scheme and on and on, it never stopped and it never has. It takes a lot to work at a football club, there are huge demands placed on staff, particularly in ticketing, it takes a huge personal sacrifice to make sure everything that needs to get done gets done but for all the difficulties that we encountered, all the tough days and nights, it was an experience that you couldn't buy, Celtic were back and it was the forefront a of the revolution. Neither Fergus, Tommy, any of the staff nor indeed the fans, would change it for the world.

It also meant that Celtic's enemies would need to up their game.

And you can read all about that in *The Asterisk Years*.

I am sure by now that the penny will have dropped.

Celtic getting stronger has weakened our enemies for sure but it has also seen them develop new ways to attack us.

Yes, Scottish Football has been on a downward spiral for years suffering from a series of major illnesses, has been on life support and has now descended into a state where it is in urgent need of lifesaving major surgery.

In *By Any Means Necessary* we discovered the extent to which the Scottish Football Association's Refereeing Brotherhood are influenced by Freemasonry and the impact that has had on providing a level playing field for Celtic for over decades with

David Syme Senior and Junior examples of anti-Celtic bias stretching back to the 1950s.

The revelations in *The Asterisk Years* stripped bare the collusion and cheating that exists at the highest levels in Scottish Society in the legal, banking, media and football worlds. These Establishment interests came together to benefit the now liquidated and extinct Rangers FC 1872 while placing all other Clubs, but particularly Celtic, at a huge sporting disadvantage.

When the lid was lifted on the Sir David Murray wheeling and dealing with the Bank of Scotland, Royal Bank of Scotland and Her Majesty's Revenue and Customs the genie was out of the bottle and no amount of behind the scenes plotting by the SFA , Rangers FC (IL) and Sevco - the Tribute Act currently operating from the Ibrox - would overcome the grassroots movement by fans of Clubs across Scotland to ensure that sporting untegrity was maintained.

Hats off to the late Turnbull Hutton who had the guts and integrity to publicly oppose the corrupt plotting of the Chief Executives of the SFA, SPL and SFL with Charles Green and Duff & Phelps to create the 'same Club' myth

The Asterisk Years also drew a parallel between the way in which standards and quality had dropped in football and refereeing in Scotland and pointed the blame firmly at the SFA for the way in which the recruitment of the National Team Managers and Referee Development Directors had been carried out and the effect that these key appointment had on training and development of footballers and referees since the 1980s.

Since 2012 our once beautiful game has been controlled by Neil '5 way agreement' Doncaster, Stewart ' Armageddon' Regan and Campbell 'EBT' Ogilvie and it is time to either declare the patient dead and buried or look for a cure and return football in this country to good health.

But Armageddon didn't happen so why change now?

Let's ask the source of this book:

"It is true that the Regan prophecy of financial meltdown only really happened to the Tribute Act at Ibrox with Hearts showing how a club can move out of administration by at least addressing their financial position and cutting their playing staff to match their income. Dundee United have returned a profit while competing at the top of the League and others are now free of bank debt.

But, the cancer at the heart of our game still exists and to settle for more of the same will simply let the usual suspects with their establishment mentality and connections continue to manipulate the system and perpetuate the 'grace and favour' Old Boy Network.

So the time is right to change how we organise and run Football in Scotland although I know that statement will bring groans of ' Oh no, not another League reconstruction!'

That is not what needs to be done.

What we should now do is wipe the current system away and look at what we would do today if we were setting up Scottish Football for the first time - not a reorganisation but a brand new fit-for-purpose system to reflect the reality of 2015 and not based on nineteenth century thinking and cronyism.

How do we go about this utopian model?

The following principles should guide development of our new system:

1) The new arrangements must be a 'bottom up' approach building from local community grassroots youth football through amateur, semi-professional (replacing the anachronistic Junior Leagues), Professional League to the Scottish National Team. Each of these levels should incorporate Women's football and provide resources to encourage participation and development of all individuals irrespective of gender.

2) Each of the above levels to have a single national governing body dealing with all Leagues within their category i.e. semi-professional to incorporate existing Junior, South of Scotland, Lowland and Highland Leagues.

3) The number of clubs participating in the professional league should be significantly reduced from the current number of 42

4) The new SFA Governing Body to carry out only essential core activities required of a National Association by FIFA & UEFA

5) Dismantle the current Refereeing structure and establish a new system to encourage recruitment and development of referees with promotion based on ability

So where do we start?

Well, to have a true bottom up structure we need to start at the grassroots level of youth football. For years, in fact decades, we have complained that we do not produce enough top class home-grown footballers. When did we last produce a regular supply of players like 'Wee Jinky', Dalglish, Baxter, Strachan, Law, ...?

The 'Largs Mafia' have coached individual skills out of our game to produce 'athletes' who will 'keep their shape' and 'track back'.

We need a system that identifies potential at a young age and nurtures and develops players through their local boys' clubs, feeding into 'Community Clubs' which in turn link to the academy system of the professional league teams.

The playing season should be changed to introduce summer football to ensure that our young players are able to train and play in conditions more appropriate to developing skills and encouraging participation.

The game at Youth level should be built around a ' Core and Cluster' model with each geographic area - City/Town/Local Authority Area - having a local development centre.

These would ideally be modelled on the current facilities in Edinburgh, Dundee, Perth, Stirling, Glasgow, Lanarkshire, Inverness, Paisley and Kilmarnock. However, until funding is available to build new Toryglen type centres, existing local Sports centres or schools should be used as the core facility.

Local youth teams and amateur teams, male and female, would be affiliated to their local core development centre with coaching development delivered locally.

Local performance development squads would identify potentially talented players who would then be streamed to community clubs and then to professional academy level.

Each development centre would be supported by the community clubs in the semi-professional leagues and the local clubs in the professional league.

A new semi-professional tier should be introduced incorporating clubs currently playing in :-

◆South of Scotland League
◆Highland League
◆Lowland League
◆Junior Football
◆Teams in SPFL who do not move to the new Professional League

A pyramid system of Regional Leagues to avoid excessive travel costs should be established feeding into a top League which would provide an opportunity for promotion to the Professional League through a Play Off at the end of the season.

When League Reconstruction has been discussed in the past, suggestions that we should reduce the number of teams in the SPL/SFL were met with the argument that teams in the lower leagues were integral parts of their communities and to remove them from senior football would be a blow to those communities.

While accepting that many clubs provide a social benefit in their community , attendances at many League One and League Two do not show a level of support which justifies maintaining a professional football club. Many of these clubs could continue to operate in a Semi Professional League with no loss of benefit to their community and in fact this could be an opportunity to develop more effective community engagement.

One of the best examples of how a club can be actively part of their community is Spartans FC in Edinburgh where their Community Football Academy is a role model which should be replicated across the country.

There should be a Community Club, operating in the Semi Professional League, based on the Spartans model linked to each of the local development centres with upwards links to Professional Club Academies.

There should be a professional league with two divisions of 12 Clubs.

The Season should run from February to December which would ensure our clubs competing in European Qualifiers in July and August are best placed to be match fit to qualify for the group stages.

Clubs will be required to satisfy criteria re ground safety, under soil heating and Financial Fair Play and require three years unqualified accounts to be admitted to membership.

Teams would play each other twice, giving 22 matches and then the teams would split into 3 groups of eight teams playing each other twice resulting in a total of 36 matches.

The top 8 in the Premiership will retain all points and play for the league title and European places.

The next group of 8 will be the bottom four clubs in the Premiership and top four in the Championship. All points up to the split will be wiped and the top four teams in the post-split mini league will play in the Premiership in the following season.

The final group of 8 will be the bottom 8 from the Championship and all points will be retained. The bottom club at the end of the season will be relegated to the semi-professional league with the second bottom club in a playoff with the second top of the Semi Pro League.

The Professional League will be governed by a Board of Directors. The PL will deal with all matters relating to their League Club Registration, Criteria Compliance, Disciplinary Procedures, Referee Appointments and Fixtures.

The CEO and Executive Directors will paid appropriate salaries and appointed through open competitive processes to attract individuals with professional skills and experience, for example Finance, Business Development and Compliance. Non-executive

Directors will be a minority of the Board and elected from member clubs.

The Memorandum and Articles of the SFA will be ripped up and rewritten to reflect the needs of the 21st Century.

The 'New SFA' will be a much leaner organisation and will be designed to deliver the core activities required of a National Association by FIFA and UEFA in terms of club and Player Registration and International Transfers and National Team participation in tournaments.

The key responsibility will be to support the development of a Football at all levels and to act as an enabling body for the sport at all levels.

It will delegate responsibility to organise the Scottish Cup and to the appointment of referees to the FIFA and UEFA Lists to the Professional League.

The SFA will appoint the National Team Manager and be responsible for all arrangements relating to National Teams.

This new SFA will remove the 'Blazers' who have for a century and a half been appointed on a 'Grace and Favour' basis from senior clubs to minor leagues and who have taken decisions with personal/club gain more important than the future of the game.

No longer will the length of time you have served be the criteria for high office which will now be based on ability, experience and skills.

Then, of course, there is refereeing.

The paranoia regarding anti-Celtic bias by referees and the SFA of which Celtic fans have been accused in the past has been shown to be fully justified in recent years with the Jorge Cadete affair, Dallas 'Pope email', Dougie Dougie, the revelations in *By Any Means Necessary* and the exposure of the Lanarkshire Referees Association in this book.

The current system of recruitment, development and promotion of Referees is clearly open to abuse and manipulation by a relatively small number of people who control all of the decision making processes and who also act as the judge and jury on any complaints raised against the organisation's members.

The system is organised on geographical County boundaries that no longer exist and all senior appointments are internally controlled with management of the Local Associations made from within the existing inner circle thus perpetuating the outdated ethos of the top end of the refereeing brotherhood.

There are thousands of genuinely motivated referees active in the youth and amateur levels of our game but as we have seen access to the senior level can be subject to control and selection based not only on ability but on other more sinister criteria.

It is time to remove control of refereeing from the Brotherhood and set up a Referee Structure that genuinely rewards ability and desire to reach the top of the profession.

The current structure should be terminated and refereeing at the grassroots should be organised at the local development centre level where all minor grades of football will be promoted and developed.

Current entrance requirements require candidates to go through an academic entrance exam which has undoubtedly deterred potential referees who have played the game, have a feel for it and know what is actually a foul or offside but struggle to pass a written exam. This is the first level that current unacceptable control is based.

Bringing in potential referees at development centres and making initial assessments on a practical basis with candidates operating at youth small sided games would encourage recruitment.

Like other walks of life where people are promoted based being the best at doing a particular job but with no account taken of managerial ability, refereeing at present is organised and managed by ex-referees.

But you do not need to have been a referee to be able to judge whether someone is making good or bad decisions. If this were the case how would the *Super Scoreboard* pundits be able to criticise referees, managers or players?

Management of refereeing at youth and amateur level would lie with the Football Development Teams at the local centres.

Using agreed assessment criteria they would regularly assess referees affiliated to their area and recommend promotion through the age groups and through the amateur leagues based on ability.

The semi-professional and professional leagues will have their own Referee Management Boards which will include ex-players, managers, other committee representatives and ex referees.

Referee Assessors will again be drawn from a cross section of individual backgrounds as above.

Promotion and demotion will be on ability.

Recruitment, training and development of referees at youth and amateur level should be managed by the Development Teams the local centres. Current and former referees could be used for practical training of new

Referee Academies should be established to develop referees who wish to progress to the Semi Professional League and then to the professional league and beyond to UEFA and FIFA levels.

Existing referees would be slotted in at appropriate levels to their current status.

Another issue that has affected the quality of referees has been the compulsory retirement age from the Senior List of Referees.

If FIFA and UEFA do not want referees on their lists over a certain age then so be it but that should not mean that all referees must be removed from the Professional List of their national Association at that age.

The two most important criteria should be a referee's ability and fitness. If a referee is still physically capable of refereeing a match at professional level and his performances are still of a high standard then he or she should not be forced to retire.

This practice has already caused standards to fall in Scotland with younger referees rushed through the lower grades to plug gaps left by experienced referees retiring. We have all been shocked at some of the performances by, for example, Norris and Dallas Junior as they were promoted too quickly beyond their ability.

So there we have it, my prescription to return the patient that we know as Scottish Football to good health.

As our beautiful game is all about opinions I am sure that you will all have your own opinions on whether some or all of this is desirable or practical.

What I hope this does is generate a genuine discussion about how we can reinvent our game and minimise the potential for unrepresentative factions to manipulate the system for their own ends or to disadvantage particular clubs and groups"

It's merely left for me to point out, despite the *Anyone But Celtic* mentality in the SFA and many other aspects of Scottish society…We Still Won.

Epilogue

I've been a Celtic supporter for 41 years now. My first gift in life was an inflatable Jinky, my first memory in life is when Andy Lynch scored a penalty against Rangers in the 1977 Scottish Cup Final, I went to my first game in 1978, have been a season ticket holder for 26 years and have seen Celtic in over 2000 games. That's not bragging, it's to point out that, although I feel qualified to talk on the subject matters raised in the three books that are part of this loose trilogy, I will inevitably be accused of bias. Of course, in this day and age, no one will say "Excuse me Sir, I put it to you that your club loyalties mean that you can't give a balanced view of this subject matter" instead abuse will come like a meteor shower. I find that I talk about abuse a lot. It is as much part of my life as food shopping and both have the same effect on me: I put up with it and it's a necessary evil I have to go through in order to do what I want to do.

I accept that I have a particular view on life, driven into me by my peers. My Father never took me to the zoo or taught me to ride a bike but he did drum into me that the ground Celtic played at was called Celtic Park not "Parkheid" , that it was Celtic versus Rangers, never the other way around, and that the colours on the Celtic scarf were the greatest in the world. So I completely recognise I am coming from a particular point of view.

Forget me though.

I know some can't and that I will be subject to abuse all my life. I believe that in Latin it is called 'ad hominem' when instead of defending a criticism against them, they turn it round and attack the criticizer.

Focus on the stuff you have read in this book.

With *The Asterisk Years*, many people told me, mainly on Twitter, what was in the book before they read the book. At film screenings many people told me they knew everything that they were about to see. To be fair, at least at screenings, all came up afterwards and admitted they were wrong.

I'm often told I should get the stuff I do out to supporters of other clubs, so they can see for themselves. Believe me I have absolutely no qualms about that. I'll sit down with anyone and talk about these things. I see my job as to try and simplify these subjects I write about as much as possible and as much for my own benefit than anyone else. I'm not here to baffle folk or do the "Joey Barton Google Search" of big words or fancy quotations every time I write something. Everything I use, I've learned already or gained from a chat with a source. That kind of research technique has been a hindrance to me also, at college they always want records of research (the SQA don't seem to give any credence to the notion that you may have gained the knowledge already).

In a time of so-called offensive behaviour at football, the only song I actually am offended by is "In your Glasgow/Aberdeen/Edinburgh/Dundee (delete as applicable) slums" It should never be a rivalry in the race to the bottom, we should all be pulling each other back up, not encouraging the type of mentality that the majority of wankers who run football clubs and authorities have now.

If I've learned one thing doing these three books in particular it is this: John Lennon was right when he wrote "They hate you when you're clever and they despise a fool"

That, more than anything, sums what the working classes have to put up with. Not that it bothers me, it makes me want to be more dedicated, get better at writing and keep doing new things but I do get plenty folk looking down on me. It was crystalized beautifully one night on the Cross Keys in Wishaw when my good friend and comrade, Jason Higgins, said "See when the revolution comes, the first place I'm going is all the golf courses and bowling clubs with the biggest shovel I can find. Dig the fucking lot of up and they'll never look down their noses at me again"

Whilst I may be partial to Golf, I recognise, respect and endorse the sentiment. Take out the upper classes who have been born and bred with an entitlement to rule and there is a layer beneath them but above us who seep their way into everything. You can go really far and say they are the reason why festivals like Glastonbury, which used to be free, now cost hundreds of pounds a ticket. For folk like us though it manifests when we try to get a better job, try and lift ourselves out of poverty, try to get fit, lose weight, get a partner who is cool or talk about subjects deemed nothing to do with us.

So we need to fight harder.

I've seen plenty who can and do fight.

I've met Celtic supporters who left Scotland, Ireland and even the Channel Islands who couldn't get anywhere on their home turf but prospered when their surname, religion and educational institution did not matter. From growing up in the cold air of persecution and in the total darkness of lack of opportunity, they now find themselves in big houses with expensive cars that have personalised 'Celtic' licence plates. Their kids have been given opportunities that many in Scotland can only dream of and they can even have a Celtic slant to their business name without any fear of discrimination. As is right. They walk the walk and talk the talk and I like that.

I was interested as well to talk to people not born into Celtic. To find out what their perspective was once they had been bitten by Celtic and all that comes with it so I spoke to a couple of guys in the situation, the first was Scott Richards who currently resides in South New Jersey:

'Don't worry about it, it's no big deal.' the calm voice said.

I thought to myself: No big deal? You're fucking kidding, right? This is why I can't watch a match outside my house! "IT WAS A GODDAMN HAND BALL!" I yelled. The "calm voice" was a fellow fanatical Celtic supporter friend of mine, who also may well have the best car in the history of the world. The hand ball in question did happen to matter, as it was what we affectionately refer to in the States as a "game changer".

The match in question was the Scottish Cup Semi-Final at Hampden versus Inverness Caley Thistle, and not one but two match officials, Steve McLean and Alan Muir (the "M" probably stands for Mason), mere yards away with only Josh Meekings and his desperation hand ball in their line of sight, refused to see what someone half way around the world plainly saw on a television. If either official properly does their job, the match for all intents and purposes goes 2-0 in Celtic's favour, Caley is down to ten men and as far as we know nobody's arse is getting trebled in Govan.

Instead, the moment is a game changer, Celtic loses and Meekings is showing off his right arm for a selfie with every jackass in the Highlands.

"If you're good enough, the referee doesn't matter." - **Jock Stein**

I love Jock.

Jock did something Rangers have never and Sevco will never do: win the biggest club trophy in the world. That being said, Jock's quote about the impact referees can have on a match is naïve at best, and at worst implies that the blame is a side's fault as opposed to placing the blame where it deserves to be placed. Worse, this quote has become the knee jerk/go to response for Tims not wanting to be perceived as whiners.

In hindsight, could Jock have really believed his own quote after watching his players get assaulted and spat upon with little to no recourse as a result of the Battle of Montevideo? Celtic had the lumps kicked out of them by Racing and responded the way a side would that was fed-up with bent officials; by taking matters into their own hands. *Is it possible I'm just seeing it wrong?*

I'm guessing no, given that Billy McNeil said as much about the officiating during the Intercontinental Cup battles years later on a Celtic TV documentary.

"Always cheated, never defeated."
As an American, I don't have to suffer the daily, childish point-scoring prattling's of the zombie horde as much as Scottish Tims. Bear in mind (pun intended), that America has made massive strides in the past twenty-five years in its passion for football, yet contrary to what any Sevconian would say, the Tribute Act has very

little following here in the States. Compared to Celtic here, their following is downright microscopic. So any interactions I have with zombies happen through social media when they troll my account.

Once, after I had ranted on Twitter about the state of officiating in Scottish football, one of the thick-as-mince troglodytes tweeted *"always cheated, never defeated"* on my timeline. Initially I laughed off the quote, just another in a long line of their inane, meaningless phrases they are so fond of.

Yawn.

After giving it more thought though, the tweet pissed me off.

I thought about how this phrase was purposely loaded. It was meant to make Celtic supporters shut up when they should be shouting at the top of their lungs.

Croppies lie down.

Be silent when Willie Collum calls for a penalty even though he never saw the foul.

Be silent when McLean cards a Celtic player for pointing out the ball isn't on the spot.

Be silent when Dougie McDougal LIED to Neil Lennon.

Be silent when Ref chief Hugh Dallas told McDougal's linesman Steven Craven to lie to Lennon and the guy refused to do so and quit instead.

Be silent when Hugh Dallas sends emails about the Pope as a threat to children.

Be silent when two officials, the same two officials that exchanged pre-match funny handshakes with each other along with the son of the guy who told McDougal and Craven to lie both stare at a blatant game-changing hand ball and refuse to call it.

Fuck. That. Shit.

The end result of all of this subversive officiating bias is a worldwide perception that the Scottish game has all of the credibility of a WWE wrestling match.

"The game's a bogey", I believe is how you guys say it.

The only thing Scottish football missing is Hugh Dallas leaving the Parthenon to come hit Broony over the head with a steel chair during the next match against the Tribute Act.

Celtic once reportedly sent a DVD of thirty suspect officiating decisions to the SFA, the "Honest Mistakes" compilation if you will. They also sent a letter to the SFA asking for an explanation for the McLean/Muir oversight. Since no response was ever made public by the SFA or Celtic, one can only surmise the letter is buried under some autographed copy of a Five-Way Agreement.

If Stewart Regan was any kind of real leader he would lay down the law with the referees and truly make them accountable for dodgy officiating with strong fines and long-term demotions. Instead, Scottish football gets a leader who apparently spends most of his days blocking Twitter accounts that ask serious and legitimate questions about lack of credibility and failed growth of the game under his tenure.

When fans know the refs by reputation better than most of the players, the game is in trouble. Yet all the Powers That Be at

Hampden seem to care about are their EBTs and ABCs: Anyone But Celtic"

*

The second was, as you probably figured I would, Graham Wilson:

"In hindsight, working out how Celtic is discriminated against in Scotland seems like an intuitive process; almost automatic. But it's not automatic. None of us are born sceptical, cynical, battle worn, and as they label us, paranoid. We all put the puzzle together in different ways, at different speeds. But the picture, once the puzzle is complete, is the same for all of us. The dirty, cheating bastards would love nothing more than to see Celtic as only a glorified sparring partner for their "blue heaven".

So how did I put my puzzle together? How big were the pieces and how quickly did I get the set complete so that I saw what was really going on? Well the first step I take in putting a puzzle together is the border. Get the outer boundary in place, then start filling in the middle. The outline was given to me by those who introduced me to Celtic. How could they not? It was the tail end of Rangers' nine in a row; the zenith of their efforts to keep us down by any means necessary. I was told of the immortal Jock Stein, during the glory years at Celtic Park, referring to the need to be good enough to overcome not just the opponent in front of you, but the officiating as well. I heard of Johnny Doyle being sent off for sending a cross in that landed square on the ref's coupon and getting sent off for it. If that was how it was in times of plenty, I can only imagine what it'd be like when tides turn for the worse.

One of the earliest experiences that I had to witness the institutionalized discrimination against Celtic was the Jim Farry arbitration hearings for delaying the registration of one Jorge Cadete. Naturally, as I picked up background about Farry and his prior dealings with Celtic, I learned of his prohibiting Celtic from playing at their home ground while it was being rebuilt and forcing the club to play at Hampden for a year and pay rent for the privilege. It could be (and was) explained the Farry was an ardent taskmaster and clinically "by the book". That same logic couldn't be applied to the Cadete affair. How could it be that a transformative player transfer could be delayed 33 days, preventing him from playing in six games, including two games against Rangers (one being a Scottish Cup tie)? I've never heard of this happening to Rangers, or any other club in Scotland for the matter.

What made this all the more shocking to me was the fact that my only exposure to sport prior to this was of American sport. The land of the free, the bastion of free market capitalism is also the home of socialized sporting structure the likes of which Trotsky would admire. The end goal of each league in every sport here is to ensure as much of a level playing field amongst member clubs as possible. This way, it's just as likely that a team from Tampa Bay can win a title, as it is from the team in New York. If anything, there's no effort to keep any one team down or lift any one team up. In theory, the worst teams get the best young players and so it goes. There is also no precedent for a technical glitch or an excuse of improper paperwork holding up a player registration. Each league oversees each transaction by its member clubs to make sure everything is done expediently and properly. And why not, better players mean better entertainment for fans watching and that is better for the league as a whole right? Well, what if there was one team that didn't fit in? What if there was one team that was so hated that you'd deliberately hamstring them so as to stunt their growth and/or prospects? Well, then you might see to it that they didn't have access to players that would improve them.

As I read of the hearings taking place looking into what happened back in March 1996, none of it made sense to me. Was I losing something in the translation? Do they have a different concept of reality in Scotland? What colour is the sky there? Oh aye, it's blue. How is it that an FA of a fellow European nation (Portugal), as well as the worldwide governing body (FIFA), send paperwork saying we are all systems go but the folks at the SFA somehow disregarding these documents as if they are making up their own rules? Are they making up their own rules to suit a particular agenda? Now ask yourself, if new rules suddenly applied which effected a member club substantially, would you not contact said club to inform them of the situation? Or would you wait a week or two to pass so that Celtic wouldn't have access to a much needed resource for arguably their biggest game of the season?

In my mind at the time, it was so blatantly obvious. How could anyone not have seen this taking place right then and there and corrected Mr. Farry to let him know he was making a mistake and holding back Celtic as well as ruining the sporting integrity of your league? As you can see, my naivety meant I had plenty more pieces of the puzzle left to fill in. But the picture was clear enough for me then as to what was taking place from the top levels and being directed at Celtic. As time went on, I stopped questioning how nobody was seeing the blatant obstacles being thrown in Celtic's way and starting acknowledging what every other Celtic supporter has known since they were wee boys and girls. The bastards are out to get us.

Jim Farry was sacked from the SFA after a decade of service and his entire tenure is marred by the Cadete affair. Wee Fergus got his revenge and cleared the record for all to see what really took place. But did it make a damn bit of difference? No, it didn't. Did it give us the last 3 months of the 95-96 season back, where our hearts were broken and Tommy Burns' (God rest his soul) hair turned white? No, the damage was done. If anything this affair gave those who'd enabled the wronging of Celtic for decades, another rod to beat Celtic supporters with. "You're all paranoid" was the only response to a scenario that ended the tenure of the top man in Scottish football. I guess when it's this obvious that something's not right, it's difficult for them to come up with a better response in the avoidance of shame. Either that or they're just thick. Probably a little of both.

When the culture is uniformly against Celtic, there must be a feeling of invincibility, where all semblance of integrity and morals go right out the window. It's a new delusional reality where institutionalized cheating is ok and no consequences can be levied for such behaviour. And that's how it went on for decades and continues to this day. The same rules do not apply for everyone, that's for sure. But it makes our victories that much sweeter. We will never need to look back and wonder how many medals and trophies we really earned. We'll never have any doubts about our own merit.

Like Fergus said

'Being a Celtic supporter is not always easy, but it is always worthwhile'

Amen to that"

Defiance from both of those guys.

I saw a lot of defiance in Las Vegas in June 2015. The embodiment of that defiance are guys Tam Donnelly and Jacky Meehan. I think, if I had to go to the trenches, then I'd like Tam at one side of me and Jacky at other. These are two guys who emigrated to Canada in the early 70s and took with them a set of street smart skills that ended up putting Celtic on the map in North America. Moreover, they helped create a staple in the Celtic calendar, the North American Federation of Celtic Supporters Clubs convention, which acts as a rallying call for Celtic supporters all over the world to come and celebrate being a Tim. Guys like Tony (Tam's brother) and Pat who I spent most of the week laughing at as they regaled me with stories that wouldn't sound out of place at a Billy Connolly gig and reminded me why, once again, I love Celtic.

In the mix is Mike Boyd, from Chicago, who adds an American twist to the Celtic cocktail.

Doing the same in Scotland, standing up for Celtic, would put an enormous target on their back. It did for Neil Lennon. It did for Aiden McGeady. How dare they be proud of who they are and where they come from. That's the attitude they faced in Scotland.

Remember how referees were recruited and what sort of professions they came from, lawyers, company owners, executives and the like. Much like The Edinburgh Establishment, it was very much them and us when it comes to refereeing.

The three targets of this trilogy I did, the press in Scotland, the Edinburgh Establishment and the Lanarkshire Referees Association were different but the same. They all lived in their own bubble and perceived themselves as untouchable. They had every right to, they were for many years.

New media and citizen journalism did for the mainstream media in Scotland. They are still around and still have plenty who both fear and believe them (unfortunately at Celtic too) but things will never be the same again and many will never trust them again. It was interesting to me how much campaigning the *Daily Record* did for the Labour Party in Scotland in the 2015 election and yet the party was massacred at the polls. This has never happened in Scotland before. People can source their news wherever they want now and little by little they are doing it more and more. This means the conditioning by the media on how people think is now getting a standing count.

Amen to that.

The Edinburgh Establishment was something I did not know even existed three years ago. I'm guessing lots of you were in the same boat. I'm also guessing most of you had no idea it was them trying to sink that boat. When I got the information on the sort of things they got up to I knew that I had to expand my mediums. That's why *The Asterisk Years* was a book that became an audio book and then a documentary. I also was faced with a problem for that project, in particular the book. I had never really written anything like it before and wondered if anyone would take it seriously. I was indebted to people that had bought my stuff previously and didn't want to just leap away from them at the drop of a hat. So I came up with an idea, a comparison piece, show my life growing up in poverty in Edinburgh and then compare it to that of the Edinburgh Establishment. A sort of juxtaposition. The factor I didn't factor in was the book sales of *The Asterisk Years* were unprecedented, the book sold six times my previous best and 70 times more than my normal stuff. This meant a whole new set of people were introduced to my work and some of them would read the book, get in touch on Twitter and say "who gives a fuck about your life?" and I accept that, no one should but I just tried to do something different. What I would say though is see if you ever read that kind of thing by anyone in the future please be assured that they didn't do it to upset you.

Quite the opposite in fact.

With *Anyone but Celtic,* I knew I would be writing very little of my own life because I didn't grow up in Lanarkshire, have never lived there and have never been a referee. Nor a mason for that matter. I also didn't really know Lanarkshire outside of the areas around its various football grounds so I needed to immerse myself in it very quickly. I realised Lanarkshire, in terms of its communities in places like Carluke, Wishaw, Cleland, Bonkle, Viewpark and Newmains to name but six was a very close knit almost overlapping place that had pockets of communities within pretty small towns. Very much like the Lanarkshire Referees Association actually. It was obvious to me, an outsider, that the masonic influence was huge in this part of Scotland, not just on refereeing, but in the structure of bowling clubs and golf clubs, their rules and even their insignia. There is also, clearly, a NRA/KKK thing going on with the Masons in Lanarkshire and the Orange Order, as one sash makes way for another and the biggest obstacle you face is remembering which hall you are supposed to be in tonight. Speak to any Celtic supporter in this part of Scotland and their experience of this kind of world is almost daily. Again, like the media and Edinburgh Establishment, the Lanarkshire Referees Association thought they could act with impunity because they always had done.

Let's hope that is about to change.

One thing I expect to be thrown at me about this book is the question "But if they are all so biased against Celtic, why have Celtic managed to win so many things? What about the Lisbon Lions? The Jock Stein era?"

It's a fair question and I will give my answer now. No matter how bad or biased referees are, good teams will be able to stop them over the course of a season. A referee can change the course of games and this has been shown in this book on several occasions but Jock Stein always said "If you want stop a referee influencing a game, score goals" The Lisbon Lions and the Quality Street Gang that came after them were pretty much invincible in Scotland for a decade. Both teams were victims of some of the most outrageous refereeing ever seen in Scotland (or anywhere for that matter) but they had players so good that they could overcome it more often than not. Indeed, with a little more luck, Celtic could have won five or six European Cups in that era.

As I have said though, one horrendous decision can derail a team. Look no further than Hampden in April 2015 and the Josh Meekings handball that referee Steven McLean (Glasgow) refused to penalise. There was clearly a lot said on the matter but, again, I thought Jason Higgins summed it up "That's why you'll never see video evidence in Scotland, because we would win the fucking treble every year"

Finally, remember also, this is the third in a loose trilogy of books and there was one deliberate theme to begin with. It would be the thing I would need to defend most of anything I've ever done. Me. *By Any Means Necessary* had a lot of me in it because I was part of the story and was telling it from my side. *The Asterisk Years* had a little less of me in it as I tried to write a parallel piece, show a life of growing up in poverty in Edinburgh and contrast that with the life of The Edinburgh Establishment. I don't regret doing that but that has given me more grief than anything I've ever done in my life. *Anyone but Celtic* has very little of my own life in it because I'm only an observer to, and commentator on, this story. I didn't grow up beside these people and I was never a referee. Yes critics, believe it or not, I do think about a book before I write it.

Again though, I have to address the situation of Celtic continuing to win trophies. The fact is when bias was at its most rife, in the 60s and 70s, Celtic had a team full of players who were born to run. They were so good that they could defeat the 14 men that they played against in most games. In the 80s, the likes of McGrain, Nicholas, McStay and Burns the talent to combine with a love of the club that ensured success kept coming and once the barren years of the 90's were over, there was Henrik.

I've also had a little bit of fun on the back of the last film and was able to use the strength of Celtic to indulge myself. One of the things that kept me going throughout *The Asterisk Years*, as the knockers and begrudgers circled like vultures eyeing a decaying body in the desert, was working away at something that started off akin to going to Mars yet ended up happening last Sunday.

The Asterisk Years screened at the Estadio Nacional in Lisbon.

It is hard to put into words what this meant to me but I'll try. It all started when a well-known Celtic legend put the idea to me back in

March. I laughed and thought it fanciful but then two wonderful guys from Portugal, Carlos and Jose, were on the case and this looked like it could actually happen. There were a few things I had to do at this end, supplying signed shirts, signed balls and various other Celtic goodies for the guys so favours were called in more than Don Corleone.

So the date was set, Sunday June 21st. Arriving at the stadium, I tried to soak it all in. It was a lovely, calm day and I was met by Carlos and Jose in the building next to the park after a short cab ride in from Saldanha. They spoke good English, which was a help obviously, but had assembled a team of entirely non English speakers.

One guy did manage a "2-1" with his fingers (at least I hope that what it was) and we moved around the running track, past the stairs where the Lions famously belted out the Celtic song, and into a sort of conference room.

I was told we had one hour and that suited me fine.

As the film started, the guys smiled but I'm not going to lie, as it went on I don't think any of them had any idea what they were watching. Also, I didn't care.

All my mind was on was getting at least one photo at the side of the park.

The film finished and a series of awkward handshakes took place akin to meeting your future in laws for the first time. After that though, the cherry on the icing, I had the run of the stadium.

The iPod was out and photos galore, loads of those ones where you're standing there and wondering why the feck the person hasn't pushed the button yet but we got there in the end.

Bliss is something I've experienced a couple of times in life and I experienced it on Sunday, for most of the day. You see the hour was in the room, I could stay in the stadium as long as I wanted and so I did. I walked round it three times, covered every blade of grass, sat in a lot of seats and stood where King Billy McNeill rose the big cup aloft and shot Celtic out in front of a race against Rangers that would end with us winning and them dying.

And so *The Asterisk Years* tour ended where the story began, in the heat of Lisbon.

Incidentally, I must pick up something here that I read just before finishing this book. Sunday Mail columnist Gordon Waddell talked about how wonderful it was to have fans of other clubs go to the Falkirk versus Inverness Scottish Cup Final. He regaled us with tales of how he watched several other teams (he being a Falkirk fan) in cup finals and other big games and said it was a crying shame that other fans didn't do the same. I think I can speak with some authority on this as I've been to a lot of games that didn't involve Celtic. I used to have a great contact at Old Trafford and took advantage of watching a very easy on the eye Manchester United team on many occasions home and away. I've been to watch games (not involving Manchester United) at Arsenal, Newcastle, Sunderland, Aston Villa, Red Bull New York and Metz to name but a few. I saw two European Cup Final's in a row in 2002 and 2003 and took in a few Scotland games too. In recent years I saw a lot of Partick Thistle and Dundee Utd, as well my share of games at Hibs

236

and Spartans. I enjoyed most of it, some of them were crap but hey ho, I love football and much prefer being there to watching on TV. Here's the thing though, I never once went to Ibrox for any game that didn't involve Celtic. Yet, out with Celtic Park, the best teams to come to Scotland played at Ibrox. Quality sides like Bayern Munich, Juventus, Ajax and Barcelona all played at Ibrox before Rangers died but I never had any inclination to go. Critics will say "Ah but you hated Rangers, you'd never go" Yet few things pleased me more than Rangers being gubbed but I still didn't go, why? I'd guess for the same reasons you wouldn't see Dr Dre at a Klan rally. People with my identity were not welcome at Ibrox for a large chunk of my life. Thousands of kids across the west of Scotland may well have wanted to see these top teams play in Scotland but if they went they would be subjected to bile for 90 minutes and nowhere did Gordon Waddell even acknowledge that.

Indeed, does anyone in Scotland in the media or in power ever acknowledge that?

I've always believed that Celtic have been persecuted in Scotland. As I said at the start of the book, I read Tom Campbell's book on the subject and whilst admiring the style of writing and level of research, I have some issues with the book and views shared by Tom, namely that we should "move on" I wouldn't criticise the book in any way but there is no way on earth Celtic supporters can or should move on from the issues that arise from bias.

Because of the many victims it leaves.

As I said right at the beginning of this book, Tommy Burns was the real inspiration behind *By Any Means Necessary: Journey with Celtic Bampots, The Asterisk Years: The Edinburgh Establishment versus Celtic* and now *Anyone but Celtic: Inside the culture that created the Lanarkshire Referees Association.*

So, with that in mind, I give the last words I leave to Simon Donnelly, who knew Tommy Burns as well as anyone: "Tommy Burns, the biggest footballing influence I had after my father. He enthused, encouraged and inspired me in my career. He seen something in me to move from centre forward to a slightly deeper role on right midfield, where I enjoyed the best time of my career alongside Jackie McNamara on the right side of a team who went a whole season and were only beaten once. It's testament to TB that the praise or comments I receive to this day are about that team, his team, bearing in mind I also played in the 1998 team that stopped 10 in a row. The Celtic fans I speak to acknowledge that season. The team epitomised him and what he wanted from his Celtic team, free flowing attacking football to excite the fans. He played and coached the Celtic way. He was the fan in the manager's shoes. When the 1995 Scottish Cup was won , as a youngster I only had to look at him, Starky, Peter Grant and the skipper, this was what it meant to older Celtic men and we youngsters looked up to that. He had foresight and a style he wanted to put over to the fans, I believe he achieved that. I, alongside many players who played under him, would say their biggest regret in football is that they never won a title for him as manager, he deserved it"

239

Bibliography

www.thecelticwiki.com
Celtic Paranoia: All in the mind? by Tom Campbell
Sports Illustrated
The Herald
The Scotsman
The Old Firm by Bill Murray
The Celtic Football Companion: by John Docherty
Wiseguy by Nicholas Pileggi

Music listened to whilst writing the book

Unknown Pleasures-Joy Division
Bummed-Happy Mondays
The Chronic-Dr Dre
Fear of a Black Planet-Public Enemy
Lethal Injection-Ice Cube
Dummy-Portishead
The Rocky Road to Dublin-The Dubliners

Thanks

This book could not have been possible without the love, support and expertise of the following people...

Douglas Young, Jock Kennedy, James Wallace, Ally Holman, David Brown, John Fallon, Joe McHugh, Mary Connaughton, Lisa Miller, Joe Bradley, Stephen McTiernan, Liam Stevenson, Danny McCambridge, Gary Bergin, Martin Wilson, James Wallace, David Harper, Joe McKenna, Jason Higgins, Richard Swan, Dougie Mooney, Michael McKeever, Johnny McKay, Simon Donnelly, John Paul Taylor, John O'Farrell, Scott and Christine Richards, Peter Meechan, Jimmy and April Olvera, Isaac and Amber Gentry, Gabriella Franco, Graham Wilson, Tommy McKeown, Chas Duffy, Kev Devine, Frankie Fraser, Brian Murray, Conor Fallon, Mick Sheehan, Ciaran Kenny, Des O'Brien, Joe Bradley, Pupster, Tim Sellick, Sean and Maeve Fitzgerald, Chris and Sandra McMonagle, Martin Lynch, Jim and Linda Kinlan, Jim Reilly, Paul Lygate, Ron Dorran, Vanessa McGuire, Andy Gordon, Davy Barclay, Paddy McOnie, Chris McOnie, Raymond Colquhoun, Frank Rafters (Father and Son).Tam Donnelly, Mike Boyd, Jose Fantingo, Carlos Fantine, Vanessa Rodriguez, Tony Donnelly, Pat Masterson and, of course, Gary Haley.